Roads Less Traveled in Northwest Oregon II

A Guide to Back Roads and Special Places

Third Edition

Steve Arndt

About the Roads Less Traveled Series:

"The series will stitch together the state's history and habitat for anyone who pays as much attention to what they're driving through as where they're going." — **Bill Monroe, *The Oregonian***

www.roadslesstraveledoregon.com

Also by Steve Arndt:

Roads Less Traveled in Northeast Oregon
Roads Less Traveled in Northwest Oregon I
Roads Less Traveled in North-Central Oregon
Roads Less Traveled in Southeast Oregon
Roads Less Traveled in South-Central Oregon
Roads Less Traveled in Southwest Oregon

Roads Less Traveled in Northwest Oregon II, Third Edition
A Guide to Back Roads and Special Places

Steve Arndt

Photographs by
Diane Arndt of Woodburn, Oregon

Maps by
Justin Eslinger, Box Lunch Design

Printed in the United States of America

ISBN: 978-0-9844294-2-4

Front Cover:
Oregon Coast near Cape Meares
(Photograph by Diane Arndt)

Back Cover (from top to bottom)
Road between Aurora and Butteville
Yaquina Bay Bridge in Newport
Champoeg Winery
Chitwood Bridge
Quartzville Creek
(Photographs by Diane Arndt)

Designed by

Justin Eslinger | Box Lunch Design
boxlunchdesign@gmail.com

Dedicated to our much anticipated first grandchild

Lia (Diane Magdalena Liani Vega)

May she inherit from us a passion for exploration and a lifelong thirst for knowledge. May she eagerly anticipate what lies beyond each bend in the road, and may she grow to have a deep appreciation of Oregon's beauty and splendor, rich history and cultural diversity.

Lia's first road trip

I shall be telling this with a sigh
Somewhere ages and ages hence:
Two roads diverged in a wood, and I—
I took the one less traveled by,
And that has made all the difference.

—Robert Frost (1874-1963)
from his poem, "The Road Not Taken"

Robert Frost's yellow wood

Acknowledgements

Special Thanks to:

The Wheeler City Manager

Walt Slayter
grandson of an early Blachly settler

Judy Gibbs
Waldport museum worker

Scott McArthur
for information about Monmouth and Bethel

Stan Hiller
long time resident of St. Paul

Harmony L. Courtney
proofreader extraordinaire

Numerous residents of Hubbard
who freely shared about their community

Merchants in Wheeler

City of Donald

City of Aurora

Independence Historical Society

Monmouth-Independence Chamber of Commerce

Pacific City Visitors Center

The Tillamook Museum and staff

Tillamook Visitors Center

Members of the Bay City Methodist Church

Teachers at Cornerstone Academy in Bellfountain

Monroe Merchants

Blachly Post office employees

Canby Museum employees

Canby Chamber of Commerce and Visitors Center

Owners of the Crow General Store

Benton County Museum workers

Peggy Dinges, Daniel's Photography; Vicki Musser, City of Woodburn; and Donna Gramse, local historian
for sharing information about Woodburn

All who provided assistance in the production of this book or shared information about their communities and with sincere apologies to anyone not mentioned by name.

Contents

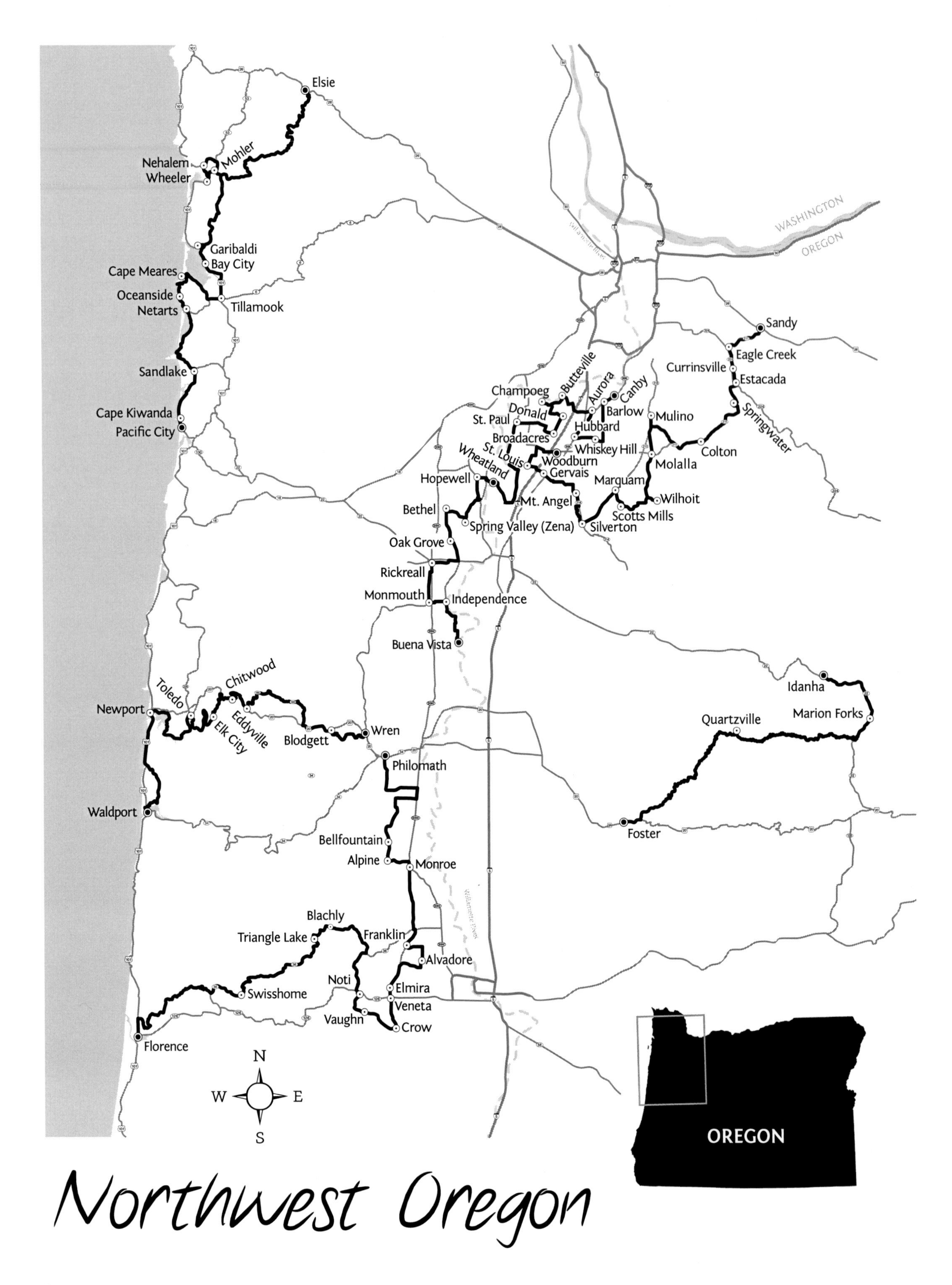

Northwest Oregon

Introduction

My wife and I are products of the 60s and 70s. The Viet Nam War, peace rallies, long hair, beards, wildly colored clothing and Annie Green Spring's wines were integral parts of the culture. A favored magazine was "Mother Earth News" which promoted a back to earth counter-culture life style that called for living off the land, raising one's own food and homesteading in the verdant mountains of Vermont and New Hampshire. Diane and I spent many hours perusing articles glamorizing the rugged, free-spirited individuals that could live off the land in the hills of New England. I distinctly remember one article in particular that told how to claim free parcels of wooded land. The requirements were simple: Improve the property and live on it continuously for three years. What could be easier!

Robert Frost's yellow wood

Pragmatism interfered with dreams and the reality of homesteading vanished, but the urge to visit the Northeast survived. Last summer we realized a thirty-year dream, traveling to New England, visiting the places we so frequently had dreamed about and envisioned.

Our trip put to rest our curiosity, both confirming and shattering three-decades of thinking. The two weeks went too quickly and we promptly learned, after encountering snow flurries in May, about the harshness of life in New Hampshire's White Mountains and the Green Mountains of Vermont. Our middle of the month travels found us staying one week at Lake Winnipesaukee, New Hampshire and one week at Smugglers Notch in Vermont. We discovered that

Introduction

spring is a non-existent season in the northeast. Summers are warm, falls are gorgeous, and winter rapidly turns into summer. We quickly learned that our unfulfilled dream of homesteading would have been an improbable, if not impossible, quest.

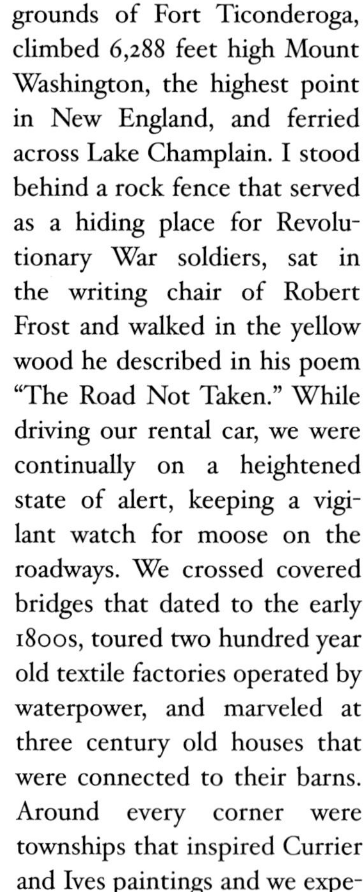

Robert Frost house

Highlights of the trip are numerous as we eagerly drove the Roads Less Traveled during our vacation. We visited homes that were built in the early 1700s, walked on the parade grounds of Fort Ticonderoga, climbed 6,288 feet high Mount Washington, the highest point in New England, and ferried across Lake Champlain. I stood behind a rock fence that served as a hiding place for Revolutionary War soldiers, sat in the writing chair of Robert Frost and walked in the yellow wood he described in his poem "The Road Not Taken." While driving our rental car, we were continually on a heightened state of alert, keeping a vigilant watch for moose on the roadways. We crossed covered bridges that dated to the early 1800s, toured two hundred year old textile factories operated by waterpower, and marveled at three century old houses that were connected to their barns. Around every corner were townships that inspired Currier and Ives paintings and we experienced the gentle action of the

Robert Frost's writing chair

Introduction

Atlantic Ocean while visiting its picturesque and quaint coastal fishing villages. We were impressed with the cleanliness of the state, seeing few abandoned cars or homes in disrepair and were very much aware that strip malls were relegated to the big cities. It was a slower life style, with warm and friendly people.

covered bridge in New England

As much as we enjoyed our visit to the northeast, we missed the diversity that our state offers. Our mountains are higher, our seasons less extreme and our coast just as rugged with greater tidal movement. Oregon, five times the combined size of Vermont and New Hampshire, has deserts, inactive and dormant volcanoes, and ghost towns, none of which exist in New England. The deepest gorge in the United States, one of the cleanest most pristine lakes in the world and wagon ruts from easterners settling in the west are prizes that we do not share with Vermont. Take time to visit the out of the way places in Oregon and learn about our state, first hand. Follow you heart and take the roads less traveled. It will make all the difference.

Steve Arndt

another New England covered bridge

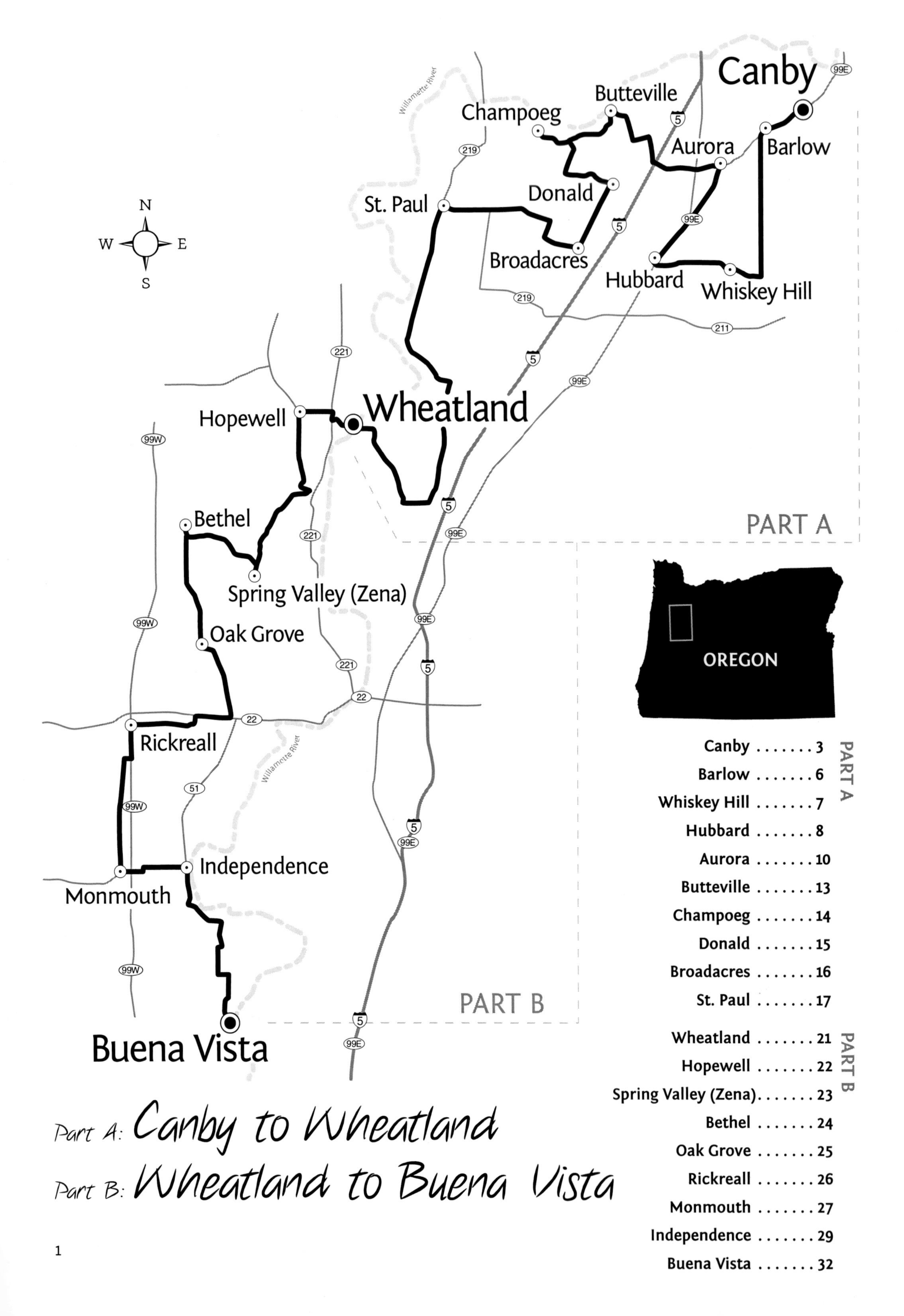
Canby
Butteville
Champoeg
Aurora
Barlow
Donald
St. Paul
Broadacres
Hubbard
Whiskey Hill
N
W
E
S
Wheatland
Hopewell
Bethel
Spring Valley (Zena)
Oak Grove
Rickreall
Independence
Monmouth
Buena Vista
PART A
PART B
OREGON
Canby 3
Barlow 6
Whiskey Hill 7
Hubbard 8
Aurora 10
Butteville 13
Champoeg 14
Donald 15
Broadacres 16
St. Paul 17
PART A
Wheatland 21
Hopewell 22
Spring Valley (Zena). 23
Bethel 24
Oak Grove 25
Rickreall 26
Monmouth 27
Independence 29
Buena Vista 32
PART B
Part A: Canby to Wheatland
Part B: Wheatland to Buena Vista

Three Ferries Across the Willamette

Part A: Canby to Wheatland (56 miles)
Part B: Wheatland to Buena Vista (40 miles)

The 309 mile-long Willamette River is the life-blood of our state and the Willamette Valley, home to more than 70% of Oregon's population. The Willamette River is one of the few rivers in the world that flows south to north, a geologic phenomena caused during the ice age when the Missoula Floods eroded the Columbia Gorge and carved the Willamette Valley.

Three ferries operate on Oregon's longest river: Canby, Wheatland and Buena Vista. For a dollar and change, cars are ushered across the river on any of these ferries. The Willamette River is used for navigation, irrigation, and recreation and played an important role in establishing Oregon City, Portland and Salem as major historical and population centers. The rich soils and the mild climate of the Willamette Valley made the area a coveted destination for pioneers, and early settlers homesteaded the fertile farmlands on both sides of the river.

Wheatland Ferry

This route begins in Canby, a short nine miles south of Oregon City, then winds through Wheatland, where Salem actually began, and concludes in Buena Vista, once famous for its fine pottery. Forty-three miles by crow, ninety-six miles by car, the route passes through many of Oregon's oldest communities.

This trip will be divided into two parts, A and B. Part A begins in Canby and the first of the three ferry landings. Part B begins at Wheatland, the location of the second ferry, and ends in Buena Vista, the third of the ferry crossings.

Part A: Canby to Wheatland

Canby

Elevation: 152 feet

Location:
45.16.000 N • 122.40.007 W

Services:
gas, food, lodging, RV, B&B

The first settler in the area was James Baker, who came to Canby in 1838 after driving cattle through the Willamette Valley from California. In 1848, Philander Lee and his wife Anna purchased land, farmed eighty acres of apple trees, and sold most of their apples to the gold-rush miners in California. In 1868, Joseph Baker settled on Baker Prairie (near the present Baker Cemetery), and opened the community's first general store. In 1870 the railroad arrived and the town was platted with streets wide enough to "drive two span of oxen and a freight wagon." The post office opened in 1888. By 1890, Canby, named for General E.R.S. Canby, who was killed during peace talks with Modoc Indians in 1873, boasted a bank, general store, blacksmith shop, department store, and three hotels. The city incorporated in 1893 and is now one of the fastest growing communities in the state.

Canby Chapel

Points of Interest

- **Site of Earthen Mound** *(NW 1st and Elm)*
  Canby was an important trading location for nomadic Native Americans. Large quantities of artifacts and the remains of a Native American fortification were unearthed here.

- **Masonic Lodge** *(288 NW 1st)*
  The lodge was built in 1912 and today is used by the Masons, Eastern Star, Job's Daughters and Rainbow Girls.

- **Canby Bank and Trust Building** *(302 NW 1st)*
  Built in 1906 by O. Roscoe Mack and known as the Arestad Building, this is the oldest bank building in Canby. A geologic marker is located in the concrete steps near the front entrance.

- **William Knight Building** *(394 NW 1st)*
  This 1890 building was constructed of hand-planed lumber. Originally, the ground floor was home to the Carlton and Rosenkrans Department Store and the upstairs housed the first City Council Chambers.

William Knight Residence

- **William Mack House**
  (139 SW 2nd)
  The founder of Macksburg (west of town), had this home built in 1879. It was completely restored in 1975 and is the second oldest home in Canby.

- **United Methodist Church Building** *(NW 3rd and Elm)*
  The tall, white-steepled church was built by Methodists in 1884 and was relocated to this spot in 1912, the year it was sold to the Catholic Church.

- **William Knight Residence**
  (525 SW 4th)
  Knight was Canby's first postmaster and later Clackamas County Sheriff. His residence, built in 1875, is one of Canby's oldest.

Canby Train Depot

- **Canby Historical Society**
  (888 NE 4th)
  The oldest commercial building in Canby, the circa 1871 train depot, was moved to its current location from Ivy and Main, where Blockbuster Video now stands. An old Southern Pacific caboose sits in front of the depot. The rail line from Portland to Canby was built by Ben Holladay and became part of the Oregon and California Railroad. The Clackamas County Fairgrounds are located adjacent to the depot museum.

- **Canby Chamber of Commerce** *(191 SE 2nd)*
  Information, brochures and a friendly staff.

- **Methodist Church**
  (NW 2nd and Elm)
  Frank Dodge built this mission-style church in 1913. The original stained glass windows were moved to the newer United Methodist Church located on Territorial Road.

- **Hoyt Brown House**
  (409 NW 2nd)
  Brown, a Southern Pacific Railroad official, built this home in 1900.

- **F.A. Rosenkrans House**
  (451 NW 2nd)
  This 1890 home was owned by one of the co-owners of Canby's first department store.

- **William Bair House**
  (375 NW 3rd)
  Bair, twice Canby's mayor, had this Craftsman home built in 1912.

- **Wait Park Block**
  (NW 3rd to 4th and Grant to Holly)
  The block was named for Aaron Wait, first chief justice of the Oregon Supreme Court, who served from 1859 to 1862. A roller skating rink once stood in the center of the park. Aaron Wait's home still stands between North Ivy and North Holly.

- **Maple Trees** *(NW 4th and Grant)*
  The Canby Civic Women's Club planted the trees between 1908 and 1925. They also planted maples on the local school grounds and in many yards around town.

- **Otto Krueger House**
  (216 NW 5th)
  Krueger, a builder of many homes and businesses in Canby, constructed this bungalow in 1910.

- **James Vinyard House**
  (290 NW 5th)
  This house was built about 1913 by James Vinyard who owned a mercantile store that stood at the corner of NW 1st and Holly. Vinyard served as Canby's mayor from 1933 until 1946.

- **Carlton and Rosenkrans Department Store**
  (181 N Grant)
  In 1912, after being in business for 21 years, Carlton and Rosenkrans built this large, modern store. At the time, it was Clackamas County's largest department store. It was gutted by fire in 1973 and is known as the Graham Building.

Canby

Points of Interest (continued)

- **Canby State Bank** *(184 N Grant)*
  Frank E. Dodge constructed this former bank building in 1912, now used by Canby Telephone.

- **IOOF Hall** *(211 N Grant)*
  The Odd Fellows Hall was dedicated in 1913 and remodeled in 1974.

- **Canby Herald** *(241 N Grant)*
  Printing Canby news since 1906.

- **Dr. White's House**
  (410 N Grant)
  Constructed in 1890, this was home to an early Canby doctor. Dr. White's son, George, opened Canby's first auto dealership (Ford) in 1911, which was located at the corner of SW 1st and Ivy (now ACE Glass shop). The dealership moved from this downtown site to its current location near the Molalla River.

- **Evangelical Church Parsonage** *(315 SE Township Rd)*
  The first Evangelical preacher occupied this home in 1876.

- **Evangelical Church**
  (339 SE Township Rd)
  Constructed in 1875 by German Evangelicals.

- **Baker Prairie Cemetery**
  (300 Block of NW Knightsbridge Rd)
  Dates to 1863.

- **Riverside School**
  (400 block of Territorial Road)
  Dates to 1907.

- **Canby Chapel** *(508 Elm)*
  This church, built in 1884 with lovely stained glass windows, is now a community chapel that is rented for private events.

- **Swan Island Dahlia Farm**
  (995 NW 22nd Avenue)
  A huge festival is held here every year, beginning the last weekend in August and extending through the first weekend in September. More than forty acres of dahlias are in full bloom during this time of year.

- **Three Rivers Ranch**
  (2525 N. Baker Drive-from Territorial, go north on Birch, turning west on 22nd Avenue)
  The more than 100-year old historic farm and barn are near the confluence of the Pudding, Molalla and Willamette Rivers.

- **Molalla River State Park**
  (go north on Holly, turning on River Park Place Road)
  Hiking trails connect the state park and the ferry landing. Ospreys frequently nest in the power poles near the landing.

- **Canby Ferry**
  (go north on Holly, turning right onto 37th, then left onto Locust Road)
  The first ferry was launched from this location in 1914. The electrically run ferry, the MJ Lee, transports passengers and vehicles across the Willamette River to Stafford and Wilsonville.

- **Zion Cemetery** *(proceed one mile east corner of Township and Walnut)*
  The first burial in this cemetery took place in 1897, with the interment of Christian Wintermantel.

- **St. Patrick's Cemetery**
  (2.3 miles east and north on Highway 99. Travel toward Oregon City, turning right onto New Era Road)
  The cemetery is more than 100 years old.

Canby Ferry

Canby to Barlow

Distance:
2.0 miles

Directions:
Go west on Knights Bridge Road to Barlow.

Points En Route

(mileage from the corner of Grant and Knights Bridge Road)

0.1 miles:
Baker Prairie Cemetery (1863).

0.5 miles:
Crossing the Molalla River.

0.6 miles:
Canby Grove Conference Center.

1.1 miles:
Turn left on S. Barlow Road.

1.7 miles:
Intersection with S. Arndt Road. Continue on S. Barlow Road.

2.0 miles:
Barlow

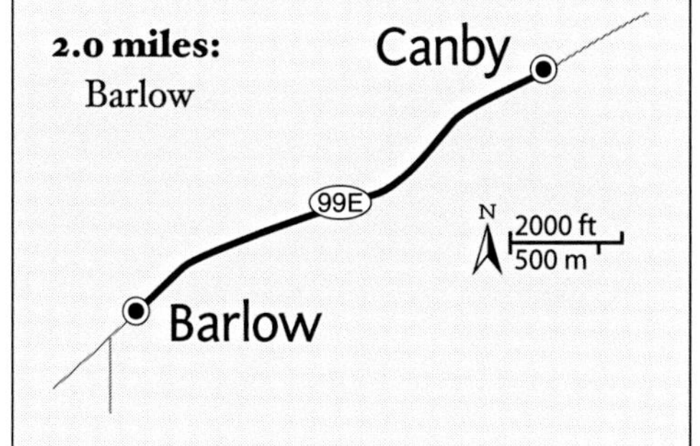

Barlow House

Barlow

Elevation: 113 feet

Location:
45.15.037 N • 122.43.354 W

Services:
none

Barlow Fountain

The community is named for Sam Barlow, who purchased the property in 1850 and then sold it to his son William in 1852. William grew the first black walnut trees in Oregon in 1859 (trees from the first shipment still line the road to his house). The railroad came through in 1870, and the post office opened in 1871. William Barlow was the postmaster from 1871-1874. He was one of the founders and early promoters of the Oregon State Fair, and owned and operated the state's first woolen mill and telegraph company. The town incorporated in 1903 and grew into an important trading center in a rich agricultural area. At one time, the community had a hotel, department store, bank, newspaper, mercantile, and freight office.

Points of Interest

- **Barlow City Hall**
  (106 N Main)
  The center of government for the almost 100 residents.

- **Barlow School** *(109 2nd Street between Maple and Oak)*
  Opened in 1905, now houses a head start program.

- **Methodist Church**
  (2nd and Maple)
  Built in 1892; the 1904 parsonage is next door.

- **Barlow Fountain**
  (2nd and Main)
  Built in 1904 to honor William and Martha Barlow, the fountain provides water for horses, people and dogs, dispensing water simultaneously at three different levels in three different bowls.

- **Barlow Cemetery**
  (S Barlow Road and King Road)
  Dates to the 1860s. Sam Barlow's grave is located here.

- **Barlow House** *(corner of Highway 99 and Barlow Road)*
  The twelve-room home, built around 1868, was heavily damaged by fire in 1884. An eighty-year old hedge, removed in the 1960s, stood on both sides of the walkway that extended from the road to the house.

Barlow to Whiskey Hill

Distance:
6.7 miles

Directions:
Go south on Barlow Road.

Points En Route

(mileage from the stop light at S Barlow Road and Highway 99E)

0.4 miles:
Concrete and gravel company.

1.3 miles:
The Zoar (Norwegian) Cemetery dates to 1892. Continue south on Barlow Rd.

3.0 miles:
Old farmhouse.

4.1 miles:
St. Joseph's Winery.

4.7 miles:
A two-story farmhouse and barn, more than a century old.

5.3 miles:
Intersection with Whiskey Hill Road. Turn right. This intersection, where a small group of homes are clustered, was once called "Ninety-One." The school in Whiskey Hill is called Ninety-One after this former community.

5.7 miles:
Century farm.

6.1 miles:
Crossing Bear Creek, named for the bears once found in the area.

6.3 miles:
Zion Mennonite Church. Many Mennonite families live in this part of Clackamas County. A cemetery is nearby.

6.7 miles:
Whiskey Hill

Whiskey Hill Store

Whiskey Hill

Elevation: 173 feet

Location:
45.10.579 N • 122.44.864 W

Services:
food, airport

Whiskey Hill, named for a still that was discovered near Rock Creek (west of the school on Whiskey Hill Road), has never been incorporated and has never had a post office. Amish and Mennonite settlers arrived here in 1876. Nearby, Rock Creek joins the Pudding River, a body of water prone to flooding.

Points of Interest

- **Whiskey Hill Store**
  (corner of Whiskey Hill Road and Meridian Road)
  Initially the 1918 school building, this store also served as the community center, gas station, convenience store, and non-denominational church.

- **Ninety One School**
  (across the street from the store)
  Much controversy surrounded the naming of the original school. Many patrons wanted the name Whiskey Hill, which opponents said was not fitting for a school. It was decided to name the school Ninety-One after the nearby Ninety-One community. The current school building was constructed in 1949.

- **Lenhardt Air Park**
  (adjacent to the school playground at 29502 Meridian Road)
  This privately-owned airport opened to the public in 1955 and has a 3,200-foot landing strip.

Whiskey Hill to Hubbard

Distance:
2.8 miles

Directions:
At the intersection of Whiskey Hill Road and Meridian Road, drive west on Whiskey Hill Road toward Hubbard.

Points En Route

(mileage from the intersection of Whiskey Hill and Meridian)

0.3 miles:
The bridge, with its unique, curved construction, spans Rock Creek, where the still was found that gave Whiskey Hill its name.

0.8 miles:
Hopewell Mennonite Church and Cemetery.

1.0 miles:
King's Industry and Nursery.

1.7 miles:
Filbert Orchards. Locals call the nut filberts, but they are better known as hazelnuts which grow world wide near the 45th parallel.

2.4 miles:
Speed zone alert.

2.8 miles:
Hubbard

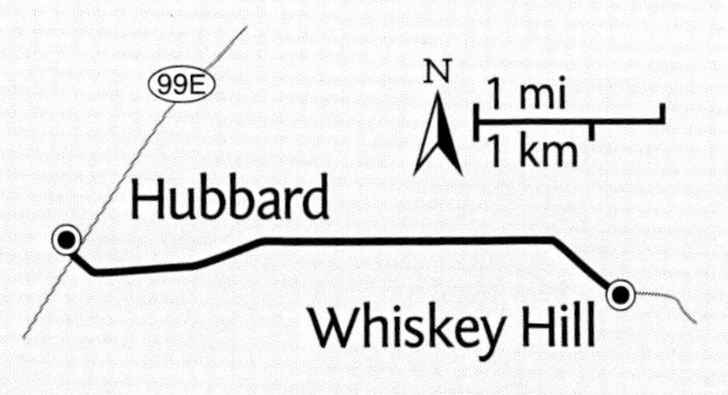

J.L. Calvert Home

Hubbard

Elevation: 156 feet

Location:
45.10.859 N • 122.48.280 W

Services:
gas, food

Hubbard was named for early settler Charles Hubbard, who came to Oregon in 1847 and built a cabin near the Pudding River. Hubbard and his family had stayed at the Whitman Mission and left for Oregon just before the Whitman Massacre. He built and operated a gristmill in the area. The first school in Hubbard was constructed in 1857 and the railroad came in 1870, which paved the way for homes and businesses along the tracks and near the depot. The first warehouse and saloon were both built in 1873. The town incorporated in 1893, with many of Hubbard's early citizens coming from Aurora's Keil Colony. Hubbard once had its own swimming pool and drive-in theater, and it has identified and labeled more historic homes and businesses than any other community in the state.

Points of Interest

- **St. Agnes Catholic Church**
  (G and Highway 99E)
  Built in 1900 and moved approximately fifty feet to its current location in the 1980s.

- **Hubbard Community Church**
  (2nd and 'I')
  Services held continually since 1893.

- **Hubbard City Hall** *(3720 2nd)*
  Dates to 1892. Portraits of every mayor hang on the walls inside the building.

- **G. Scholl House** *(3129 3rd)*
  Brother to J. Scholl, G. Scholl built this home in 1910.

Hubbard

Points of Interest (continued)

- **J Scholl House** *(3169 3rd)*
  Built in 1890, this home is one of Hubbard's oldest.

- **Mary Goudy House** *(3189 3rd)*
  Constructed in 1915.

- **Dr. E. Schoor House and Office** *(3249 3rd)*
  The addition on the side of his 1920 home served as his dental office.

- **Hubbard Inn** *(3389 3rd)*
  This restaurant has served food since 1898.

- **Homestead Restaurant** *(3519 3rd)*
  Built in 1881 as the Commercial Hotel. Only one story remains from its original design.

- **Hubbard Drug Store** *(3559 3rd)*
  Built in 1895 by Mr. James, this was the community's second such store.

- **Hubbard State Bank** *(3589 3rd)*
  Constructed in 1910, the building now houses the ReMax Realty office.

- **W.R. Hurst House** *(3737 3rd)*
  Built in 1890.

- **Rose Jordan House** *(3789 3rd)*
  Constructed in 1903.

- **August Will House** *(3849 3rd)*
  Built in 1912, Will had a successful general merchandise store in Aurora.

- **Home of Charles Mayger** *(4199 3rd)*
  This house was constructed in 1908.

- **B. Paulsen Residence** *(G and 4th)*
  1917 construction.

- **Charles Stahl House** *(3227 4th)*
  This home was built in 1910.

- **George Knight House** *(3427 4th)*
  The 1905 home of George Knight, relative of William Knight of Canby.

- **Hubbard City Park** *(between 4th and 5th and D and E)*
  The park spans one full city block. Restrooms, picnic area and playground equipment.

- **W.S. Buchanon House** *(3124 5th)*
  1887 construction.

- **H. Scholl House***(3284 5th)*
  Several members of the large Scholl family built homes in Hubbard, including this one built in 1870 by Henry Scholl.

- **The Fry House** *(3375 5th)*
  Built in 1908. The Fry's had a successful business in Aurora.

- **Charles Kinzer House** *(3532 5th)*
  Constructed in 1885, this is one of Hubbard's oldest homes.

- **J.L. Calvert House** *(3635 5th)*
  Occupied since 1895.

- **George Domick House** *(3735 5th)*
  The 1903 home of an early Hubbard merchant.

- **R.C. Painter House** *(3390 7th)*
  The 1888 home of one of Hubbard's earliest settlers.

Hubbard Drug Store and State Bank

- **Dr. Weaver House and Clinic** *(2899 A)*
  Weaver was the first doctor in Hubbard. He built this home in 1886, later adding rooms that served as his clinic.

- **C.M. Crittenden House** *(2495 C)*
  One of Hubbard's more ornate homes, built in 1905.

- **Pythian Building** *(3rd and F)*
  This building also houses Kreigsco Industries. The Order of Pythians began in the United States in 1864, emphasizing "Friendship, Charity and Benevolence."

- **Platz House** *(2629 F)*
  The Platz's, some of Hubbard's earliest settlers, built this home in 1885.

- **L.M. Scholl House** *(2670 E)*
  Once the home to one of Hubbard's Mayors, it has been occupied since 1908.

- **B. Paulsen House** *(2737 G)*
  Built in 1917.

- **A. Jordan House** *(2770 J)*
  One of Hubbard's older homes, built in 1883

- **Hubbard Water Tower** *(next to the fire station on 2nd between H and I)*
  Erected in the 1940s, replacing a wooden tower that stood on the same location.

- **Barendse Park** *(off 5th and Allen)*
  Skate park, ball fields, soccer fields, restrooms, picnic area and playground.

- **Hubbard Mineral Springs** *(northwest on Mineral Springs Road)*
  A source of geothermal heated water that drew people for therapy and swimming. Today it is private property.

Aurora

Elevation: 156 feet

Location:
45.13.888 N • 122.45.277 W

Services:
gas, food, B&B, RV

Old Aurora Colony Museum

Settled in 1856, Aurora began as a religious utopian community originally named Aurora Mills for the daughter of founder Dr. William Keil. The Aurora Mills post office opened in 1857 and the railroad came in the late 1860s. Each day, four trainloads of passengers stopped to enjoy the excellent meals at the Colony Hotel. Aurora Mills was a highly successful society where the communal members exemplified the golden rule and lived the credo "each according to his ability and to each according to his need." The colony was known for its industriousness, quality of product, good food, hospitality, and music. Keil came to Oregon from Willapa Bay, Washington, where he attempted to establish a similar, religious, utopian community. Keil's son, Willie, a sickly lad, was too ill to make the westward trip. Upon Willie's deathbed, Dr. William Keil swore to his son that he would take him overland to the west coast. Fulfilling the promise, Dr. Keil transported his son's body in a whiskey filled, lead-lined coffin, and buried Willie in Willapa. Dr. Keil died in 1877 and the communal society dissolved by 1883. In 1894 the name was shortened to Aurora. Today, Aurora is famous for its antique stores. Several fires have taken their toll on many of the old buildings and historic homes.

Points of Interest

- **The Old Aurora Colony Museum** *(2nd and Liberty)*
  The museum is comprised of several buildings; the 1862 Ox Barn, the1864 Kraus House, the 1876 Steinback Cabin, and the 1877 Summer Kitchen. The Aurora Colony Historical Society converted the Ox Barn into a museum in 1966. Each building is filled with artifacts from the settlement, known as "Oregon's only successful communal society."

Hubbard to Aurora

Distance:
3.5 miles

Directions:
At the intersection of Highway 99 and D Street, drive north on Highway 99.

Points En Route

(mileage from the traffic light)

1.4 miles:
Intersection with Stauffer Road, named for early, prominent Hubbard citizens. The 1870 Stauffer Home can be found approximately 0.6 miles down Stauffer Road. Square nails were used to construct this historic home.

1.6 miles:
Stay right on Highway 99E toward Aurora and Oregon City. The road parallels the railroad tracks all the way to Aurora.

3.0 miles:
A row of cedar trees, planted over one hundred years ago, welcome travelers to Aurora.

3.5 miles:
Aurora

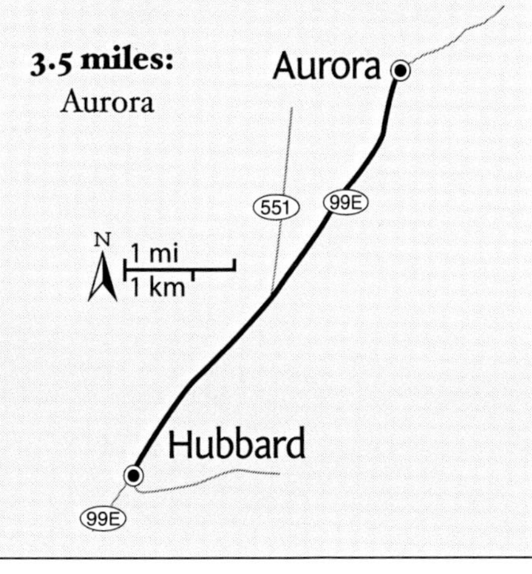

Aurora

Points of Interest (continued)

Depot Antiques

- **Christ Lutheran Church**
  (off Liberty on 2nd)
  Built in 1899, several additions have been made to the building. There is a time capsule placed near the front of the church where it is scheduled for opening in 2099.

- **Jacob Miller House** *(15009 2nd)*
  Constructed in 1890, this is one of the larger, more ornate homes in town.

- **George Smith House**
  (15058 2nd)
  Dates to 1870.

- **Christian Zimmerman House**
  (21514 2nd)
  Erected in 1900. Note the tree that stands in front of this old home, planted when the home was built.

- **Leonard Triphena-Will House**
  (21533 Liberty)
  1905 construction. Will was co-owner of Will Brothers Bazaar, a large general merchandise store that is now a three-story antique mall.

- **Henry Kraus House** *(21544 2nd)*
  The second home for the Kraus family was constructed in 1900.

- **Aurora Presbyterian Church**
  (between 2nd and 3rd on Liberty)
  This church, built in 1913, replaced the 1880 building. The 1880 church building served as the Aurora Mills Colony School. Inside the church is a 1915 Henners Track Pipe Organ. It is the only instrument of its kind in the state and is still in use. The hand made pews are held together with square nails made in the old colony.

- **Will-Snyder Store**
  (2nd and Main)
  Opened for business in 1912. The building now houses three floors of antiques.

- **Octagon Building**
  (2nd and Main)
  Circa 1865, this unusually shaped building is the only remnant of the old Aurora Hotel. The hotel stood near the present site of the community restrooms.

- **William Fry House**
  (2nd and Main)
  Dating to 1874, the home is now an antique store.

- **Walter Fry House** *(next to William Fry home on Main)*
  Walter was the younger brother to William. His home was constructed in 1900.

- **Jacob Miley House**
  (behind the Fry homes)
  Constructed in 1865, it serves as another of Aurora's antique stores.

- **Moehler House** *(18877 Main)*
  1856 construction.

- **Fosmark House** *(21551 Main)*
  Home of Dr. Geisey, local doctor. His name is etched in the glass of the front door. Look for an interesting mileage marker in the corner of this property.

- **Aurora Colony Store**
  (21581 Main)
  The old colony store opened in 1871.

- **Aurora Train Depot**
  (21651 Main)
  The 1870 train depot has been converted to an antique store. Old train memorabilia is displayed around the outside of the building.

Aurora elevator

- **Old Aurora State Bank** *(21690 Main)*
  Now the Pheasant Run Wine store. The old vault can be viewed inside the store.

- **Victorian House** *(14996 3rd)*
  An old two-story home near the museum.

- **Old House** *(21513 3rd)*
  Lots of gingerbread can be seen on this turn of the century home.

- **Aurora Grange Hall** *(3rd and Main)*
  The current location of frequent craft sales and bazaars.

- **Remember When Antiques** *(21527 Highway 99E)*
  Converted into a store and restaurant, this building was one of the first homes constructed following the 1877 death of Dr. Keil.

- **Pacific Hazelnut Candy Factory** *(14673 Ottoway Ave)*
  Candies, jams, jellies, nuts and free samples.

- **Irvin Family Cemetery** *(located in a fir grove within the Weyerhauser Tree Farm, 0.6 miles north of Aurora)*
  The cemetery is located on an 1850 donation land claim staked by the Irvin family. The Irvin home, which stood near the family cemetery, was built in 1852 and destroyed by fire in 1969.

Aurora to Butteville

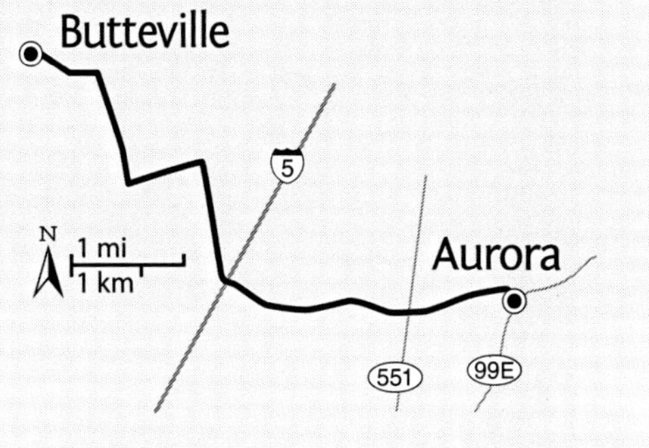

Distance:
6.8 miles

Directions:
From corner of Highway 99E and 1st, go west onto Ehlen Road toward Butteville.

Points En Route

(mileage from the traffic light at 99E and 1st)

0.1 miles:
Crossing Mill Creek.

0.5 miles:
Cole Road. Dr. Keil is buried in the family cemetery at the end of this lane.

0.9 miles:
Oak Lane. At the end of this road is the 1860s Aurora Colony Cemetery.

1.0 miles:
Stoplight and intersection with Hubbard-Wilsonville Road. Continue on Ehlen, crossing the highway.

1.2 miles:
Crossing Boones Ferry Road, named for Daniel Boone's grandson, a ferry operator.

1.6 miles:
Holly farm.

2.7 miles:
I-5 underpass.

2.8 miles:
Turn right on Bents Road, which is located near the truck stop. Drive north.

3.7 miles:
Turn left on Fargo Road.

3.8 miles:
Fargo: An old gas station near the railroad tracks at Yeary Lane. The old school house, which stood nearby, was torn down in March of 2007.

4.3 miles:
Turn right on Schultz Road.

5.2 miles:
Intersection with Arndt Road. Stay on Schultz.

5.8 miles:
1836 Butteville Cemetery, one of the oldest in the state. Relatives of Daniel Boone are buried here.

6.1 miles:
Intersection with Butteville Road. Turn left. Look for old farmhouses intermingled with newly constructed mega homes.

6.8 miles:
Butteville

along the road from Aurora to Butteville

Butteville

Elevation: 136 feet

Location:
45.15.710 N • 122.50.522 W

Services:
food (if store is open)

former Butteville Boys Home

Named by French trappers as early as 1821, Butteville, located on the Willamette River, received its name from La Butte, a hill that rises about one mile from the store. The town was platted in 1850. The post office opened the same year and closed in 1905. Daniel Boone's grandson had a ferry service five miles east, where today's I-5 bridge crosses the Willamette River. Boone's grandson's grave marker reads, "Here lies a woodsman of the world." Floods have destroyed many of the older homes around Butteville, the worst damage occurring in 1861.

Points of Interest

- **Butteville Store**
  (10767 Butte Street)
  One of the oldest stores in Oregon, it was opened in 1863 by Francis X. Matthieu, who traded beaver belts for grain and supplies with the Champoeg Indians. J.J. Ryan purchased the store from Matthieu and promptly built a tavern that stood next to the store. The store is currently owned and operated by the Oregon State Parks. An antique cash register similar to those used more than a century ago rings up sales.

- **Garage across from the Store**
  (Butteville Tavern)
  Allegedly, this old garage housed Butteville's first Tavern.

- **Historic House** *(across from the store on Butteville Road)*
  In the early 1900s, this large farmhouse served as the Butteville Boys Home.

Butteville to Champoeg

Distance:
3.5 miles

Directions:
From the Butteville General Store, turn right onto Butteville Road.

Points En Route

(mileage from the general store)

0.4 miles:
Turn right on Champoeg Road. Hazelnut orchards and hops line the route.

0.9 miles:
Champoeg Cellars and Wine Tasting room.

2.3 miles:
Intersection with Case Road. Proceed on Champoeg Road.

2.5 miles:
Crossing Champoeg Creek.

2.9 miles:
Zorn House, 8448 Champoeg Road, was constructed about 1870. Tours are given the second Sunday in June. The current owners are descendants of Casper Zorn, first resident. An unusual bell tower and barn stand across the street.

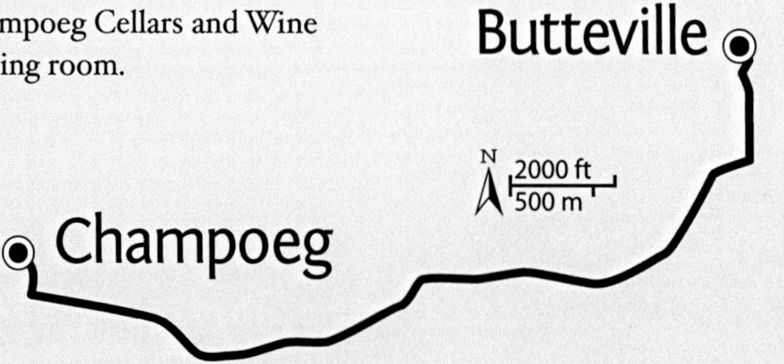

Champoeg

Elevation: 136 feet

Location:
45.14.925 N • 122.53.809 W

Services:
none

The town was originally platted in what is now the state park. Most of the town's 200 residents lived where the park's pet exercise area and the DAR Museum are currently located. The first permanent settler was John Ball, who came to the area in 1833. In 1841, the Hudson's Bay Company built a warehouse here. In 1843, Joe Meek called for the famous provisional government vote, which passed 52-50, making Oregon a U.S. territory (a marker designates the site). The post office opened in 1850, and Robert Newell and Andre Longtain platted the town in 1852. Major flooding devastated the entire community in 1861. The post office closed in 1905. Wooden posts identify the street names of the former town. Near the granite memorial in the state park stands a covered area that shows how high the water reached during the 1861 flood. The Champoeg Schoolhouse, built after the 1892 flood, is a private residence and located on Jette Court.

Champoeg Winery

3.3 miles:
Entrance to Champoeg State Park. (DAR and State Museums) Interpretive Center, full hook-ups for trailers, cabins, camping, and yurts, picnicking, boating, fishing, biking and hiking trails.

3.4 miles:
Newell House Museum entrance. A reconstructed 1850s home, the complex includes the old Butteville School and jail. Worth the stop! The Belle Passi Chapter of the Daughter's of the American Revolution meets here on a monthly basis.

3.4 miles:
Intersection with French Prairie Road. Turn right, staying on Champoeg Road.

3.5 miles:
Champoeg

Zorn House

Points of Interest

- **Champoeg State Park Interpretive Center** *(near park entrance on Champoeg Road)*
  The park opened in 1912 and gained State Park status in 1943.

- **DAR Museum**
  (near the river inside the park)
  The museum was constructed in 1931, near the site of early settler Donald Monson's home that fire destroyed in the same year.

- **Robert Newell House**
  (8089 Champoeg Road)
  Newell was Oregon's first speaker of the House.

- **Champoeg Cemetery**
  (off Case Road)
  Dates to the 1840s and is one of the oldest in the state.

Champoeg to Donald

Distance:
4.8 miles

Directions:
From the Newell House and the intersection of French Prairie Road and Champoeg Road, go left on French Prairie Road traveling toward St. Paul.

Points En Route

1.1 miles:
Turn left on McKay Road.

1.9 miles:
Champoeg Creek.

2.1 miles:
Crossing Arbor Grove Road. Continue on McKay Road.

2.8 miles:
Intersect with Case Road. Continue on McKay. To the right, on Case Road, is the 1850 Case farmhouse, the oldest ranch-style home in Oregon.

4.7 miles:
Turn right on Donald Road.

4.8 miles:
Donald

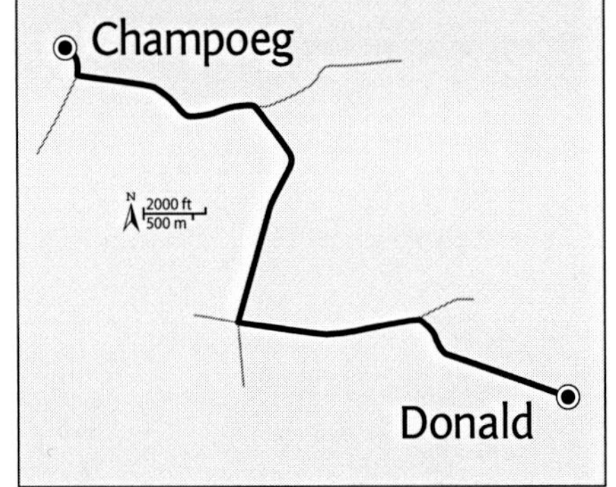

Donald

Elevation: 171 feet

Location:
45.13.349 N • 122.50.354 W

Services:
gas, food, B&B

Donald was named for R.L. Donald, construction supervisor for the Oregon Electric Railroad that passed through town in 1908. Donald was a close friend of Henry Zorn, who owned much of the land that today comprises the town. The old Oregon Electric booster station still stands near the tracks adjacent to the Donald Farmer's Co-op. Many older homes line Main Street and Butteville Road, as well as Oak, Matthieu, and Ehlen Streets.

Electric Railroad Booster Station

Points of Interest

- **Donald Store** *(10750 Main)*
  This store was constructed in 1918.

- **Old Mercantile Building** *(10760 Butteville)*
  Owned by H.B. Evans, the building housed the city's first post office.

- **Donald City Hall** *(10790 Main)*
  1912 construction. Many old pictures are displayed inside.

- **Donald Tavern** *(10791 Main)*
  This 1906 building was originally the Mays and Good general mercantile store. It became a tavern in 1935. The old livery stable, razed in the 1950s, stood behind this building.

- **Masonic Lodge** *(10801 Main)*
  The Lodge occupied the upstairs of the 1915 Hoskins/Desart building; the downstairs housed the bank and a general store.

- **Glade Building** *(10821 Main)*
  Constructed in 1923, it was home to the Butteville Insurance Company and the Donald Bank. Henry Zorn was the first bank president and owned a large home near Champoeg Park.

- **Electric Railroad Booster Station** *(10860 Main)*
  The 1912 Oregon Electric Terminal and booster station lies vacant, someday to open as the Donald Historical Society.

- **Flag Pole** *(Williams and Main)*
  Erected in honor of Lieutenant Albert A. Lamb, Donald resident who was killed in the bloody WWI Battle of Argonne on October 14, 1918.

- **Boyer Market** *(Main and Butteville Road)*
  This small grocery store, an add-on to the owner's home, was built in the early 1900s.

- **Donald School** *(Main and Butteville Road)*
  This school building, constructed in 1938, replaced the 1911 school, which burned.

- **Donald Cooperative Cheese Factory** *(Main and Crissell)*
  Widely known for its excellent fromage blanc.

- **Donald Brick and Tile** *(two blocks south on Mathieu)*
  The tile factory, near the railroad tracks, opened in 1911 and closed in 1985.

- **Donald City Park** *(Feller and Main)*
  Some playground equipment and a portable toilet.

- **Donald Skate Park** *(Main near the railroad tracks)*
  Here skaters go down a 9-foot crater known as "the pool." This was Oregon's first such structure, built at a cost of $35,000.

Donald to Broadacres

Distance:
2.7 miles

Directions:
At Main and Butteville Road, go south toward Broadacres. Many old and interesting farms and barns line this road.

Points En Route

(mileage from the intersection of Main and Butteville)

0.2 miles:
This 1890 Victorian home is one of Donald's earliest residences.

0.7 miles:
A family nursery and remnants of a windmill.

1.3 miles:
Old farmhouse with a unique water tower and interesting barns.

1.5 miles:
At the corner of Olmstead Road and Butteville Road is the 1896 Fred Miller home next to an 1893 hop barn.

2.3 miles:
Crossing railroad tracks.

2.7 miles:
Broadacres

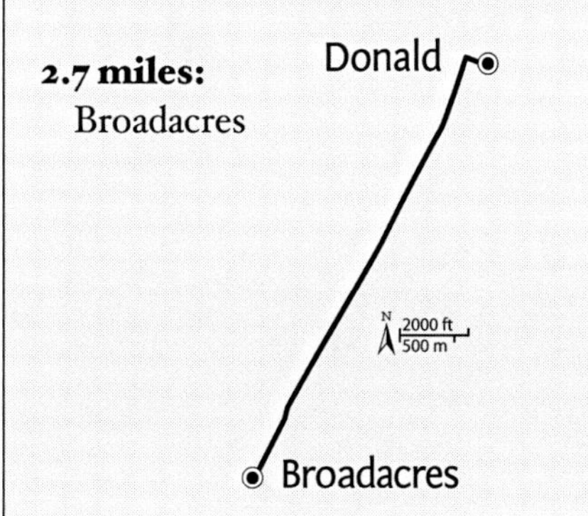

Broadacres

Elevation: 171 feet

Location:
45.11.274 N • 122.52.109 W

Services:
food

Located at the intersection of Butteville Road and Broadacres Road, the community of Broadacres sprang to life after the 1908 Oregon Electric Railroad laid track here. A few older homes still exist west of the intersection. Broadacres' name is derived from the broad expanse of farmland through which the tracks were laid.. The Broadacres post office opened in 1914 and closed in 1928. The old general store and tavern form the hub of the small farming community.

Points of Interest

- **Broadacres Store and Tavern** *(intersection of Butteville Road and Broadacres Road)*
  The building was constructed shortly after the railroad began stopping in Broadacres. The upstairs was a dance hall.

Broadacres Store and Tavern

Broadacres to St. Paul

Distance:
6.2 miles

Directions:
Drive west from the Broadacres Store and Tavern.

Points En Route

(mileage from the intersection of Butteville and Broadacres)

0.1 miles:
1914 Broadacres School, which has been remodeled into a community church.

1.0 miles:
Case Creek, which was named for an early Champoeg area pioneer. Nursery stock, hops, and hazelnut orchards are in the area.

1.4 miles:
Arbor Grove Road. Turn right.

2.0 miles:
Turn left on the St. Paul Highway.

3.2 miles:
Crossing Champoeg Creek.

4.5 miles:
Intersection with French Prairie Road (Highway 219). Continue west.

6.0 miles:
The Kirk House. Brothers John and Thomas built this spacious home in 1882. The circular front entrance was added later.

6.1 miles:
Swale. Year-round bass, crappie, and bluegill fishing.

6.2 miles:
St. Paul

219
St. Paul
N
1 mi
1 km
219
Broadacres

Kirk home

St. Paul

Elevation: 185 feet

Location:
45.21.211 N • 122.97.676 W

Services:
gas, food

French Canadian fur trappers were the first area residents, coming in the 1820s. In 1839, pioneer missionary Francis Blanchet established the St. Paul mission here. The community is named for the Apostle Paul and the post office has been operating since 1874. The town incorporated in 1901. St. Paul is home to the St. Paul Rodeo, held every Fourth of July. The rodeo grounds occupy much of the community's core area. St. Paul is an agricultural community where a wide variety of commercial crops are grown.

Points of Interest

- **St. Paul Catholic Church**
  (Blanchet and Christie)
  The existing church dates to 1846 and replaced the original 1839 log cabin structure. A replica of this structure sits next to the 160+ year old structure. Over 300,000 bricks were used in the construction of the church and all of them were made from local clay. In the floor of the church are several 1840s graves. Father Blanchet celebrated the first mass on January 9, 1839.

- **Old St. Paul Cemetery**
  (on Main across from Convent)
  A brick wall commemorates the 546 people buried here. Names are on plaques affixed to the wall. William Cannon, Oregon's only Revolutionary War veteran is buried here. The first burial occurred in 1839.

- **St. Paul Cemetery**
  (6th and Highway 219)
  Dates to the 1870s and is the final resting place of Francis Blanchet, Oregon's first Archbishop, who died in 1883. A mortuary chapel once graced the back of the cemetery where it overlooks the creek, but was removed in 1939. A monument marks the site of the chapel. The cemetery is the site of the first church. The old, log structure was constructed here in 1839 and a replica stands next to the St. Paul Church. Joseph Gervais, founder of Gervais, is buried in this cemetery.

- **Site of St. Joseph College**
  (next to the cemetery)
  A boarding school opened here in 1843 and flourished until 1848, when most of the men and boys went to work the gold fields in California. It became a hospital in the 1850s, but fell into ruin and eventual decay. A few scattered and broken bricks mark its location.

- **St. Paul Rodeo Grounds**
  (between Main and 5th on Malo)
  Thousands of rodeo fans attend this annual Fourth of July event.

- **Old Houses**
  (between 2nd and 3rd on Mission)
  One of these three homes belonged to Emmett Kirk and once housed the St. Paul historical society. All three of these structures were moved here from their original locations.

- **Site of the Willamette Academy**
  (MacDonald and Convent)
  The girl's school, run by six nuns, operated from 1844 to 1853.

- **US Bank** *(between Blanchet and Church on Highway 219)*
  This operating bank is located in an old concrete-block building. Next door to the bank is the St. Paul community center.

- **St. Paul Community Center**
  (20239 Main)
  Constructed in 1938 as a WPA project.

- **Matthew Murphy House**
  (behind Twin Oaks)
  This home was moved to its current location from near the river off of Mission Road. One of the bricks in the chimney is dated 1832.

- **St. Paul Creamery**
  (across from the grade school softball field on Highway 219)
  The old brick building stands next to the old cemetery.

St. Paul Catholic Church

St. Paul Creamery

St. Paul to Wheatland

Distance:
17.3 miles

Directions:
From Main and Park, drive south on Main Street, also called River Road.

Points En Route

((mileage from Main and Park) Look for numerous old homes, barns, orchards, and farms along this route.

0.4 miles:
Century-old farmhouse and outbuildings. (19751 River Road)

1.1 miles:
This farm is more than 100 years old.

1.4 miles:
Old barn.

2.4 miles:
A large, old willow tree.

3.6 miles:
LDS cannery and warehouse.

5.3 miles:
Century Farm.

7.1 miles:
The Byrd House, constructed in 1870.

7.3 miles:
The Fairfield Cemetery is located near the trees about 0.5 miles north.

7.5 miles:
1929 Fairfield Grange. The community of Fairfield was settled in the 1850s, had its own post office in 1852 and a general store in 1856. Before the railroad, it was an important shipping point for river freight. Little remains of this community.

7.8 miles:
Newsom Orchards and intersection. Turn right onto River Road and drive south.

9.1 miles:
The old Eldridge School, now Salem Bible College.

10.0 miles:
Old farm.

10.6 miles:
The former Waconda School, at 4161 Egan Road, has been a private residence since 1977.

10.7 miles:
Waconda. The community grew when the Oregon Electric Railroad built a booster station here. The old cement structure still stands about 0.4 miles east on Waconda Road. Waconda had its own post office in 1912. A few homes and an abandoned store remain from better days.

12.5 miles:
Hopmere, formerly called Chemeketa, is another small community that flourished and died along the Oregon Electric Rail Line. The name was changed to Hopmere, as many acres of hops, a major cash crop in the early 1900s and vital ingredient in making beer, were grown here. Artificial ingredients in the production of beer have resulted in the reduction of the number of acres planted since hop production reached its peak in the 1930s.

Waconda Electric Railroad Booster Station

Waconda School

12.5 miles:
Intersection of River Road and Brooklake Road. Turn right and drive west on Brooklake.

13.6 miles:
Intersection with Wheatland Road. Turn right and drive north. These bottomlands are prone to frequent and major flooding.

14.5 miles:
Old farmhouse.

16.0 miles:
Willamette Mission State Park. The park is the site of the 1834 Willamette Mission, established by the Reverend Jason Lee, who preached to the pioneers and the Native Americans. Lee built a one-room log Mission House, which functioned as a school, chapel, hospital, kitchen and living quarters. A barn and second room were completed by 1836. Additional emigrants arrived in 1837, including Anna Pittman, whom Lee took for his wife. A blacksmith shop, granary, and hospital were added to the complex by 1839. This location was abandoned in 1840 in favor of Salem, near today's Willamette University. The great flood of 1861 severely damaged the mission buildings and changed the course of the river. The site of the first mission can be viewed in the park by hiking the Mission Monument Trail. The park has boat ramps, fishing docks, and 12 miles of trails (jogging, bike, hike, and horse) including a 2.5-mile self guided walking trail. Also available are camping, both family and group, that can accommodate over 100 campers. Numerous native species of birds and animals can be seen from two wildlife viewing areas. An estimated 270-year old Black Cottonwood, the nations largest, stands on the bank of Mission Lake. From the park, return to Wheatland Road, and continue north to Wheatland and the ferry.

16.8 miles:
Turn left on Matheny Road, heading to the ferry.

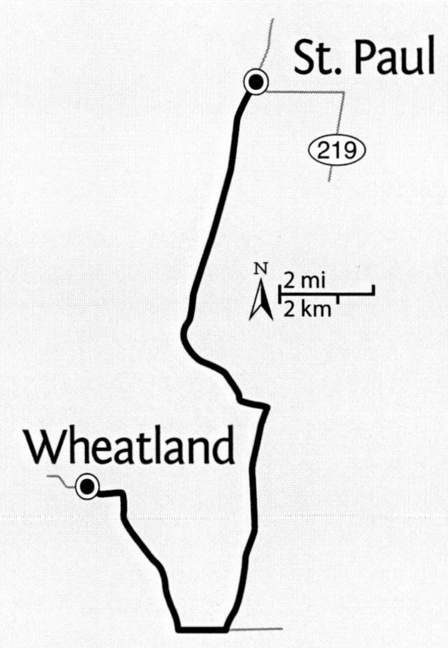

17.1 miles:
Willamette Mission Park Boat Launch.

17.2 miles:
Wheatland Toll Ferry. At this location in 1844, Daniel Matheny operated the first toll ferry. Marion and Yamhill Counties took control of the toll ferry in 1936, christening the fifth ferry in 2001. Over 225,000 vehicles use this ferry each year. Take the ferry across the river to the site of Wheatland.

17.3 miles:
Wheatland

Hops growing near Willamette Mission

Wheatland Toll Ferry

Part B: Wheatland to Buena Vista

Wheatland

Elevation: 171 feet

Location:
45.05.503 N • 123.03.017 W

Services:
none

Nathaniel Matheny came to Oregon in 1843 and in 1844 built one of the first ferries to cross the Willamette River. In 1847, Matheny founded the town of Atchison City, whose name was changed to Wheatland in the 1860s. The post office opened in 1867 and closed in 1903. Wheatland once boasted 319 residents, a school, church, two hotels, and a dozen businesses. A historical marker stands in front of one of the few existing homes.

Points of Interest

- **Arcane Cellars at Wheatland Winery** *(22350 Magness Road NW)* Located above the banks on the west side of the Willamette River near the Wheatland Ferry landing. Tasting room open weekends year-round.

Wheatland to Hopewell

Distance:
2.5 miles

Directions:
From Wheatland, travel west toward Maud Williamson State Park.

Points En Route

(mileage from the historical marker in Wheatland)

0.9 miles:
Intersection of Wheatland Road and Highway 221. Turn right and travel north.

0.9 miles:
Maud Williamson State Park. Covered area, picnic, restrooms and a grove of old-growth firs. An old home, built during the Civil War and now a private residence, stands near the entrance to the park.

1.1 miles:
Turn left, heading west on Lafayette Highway. This is called Pine Tree Corner.

2.2 miles:
Old farmhouse.

2.4 miles:
Hopewell Church.

2.5 miles:
Turn left on Hopewell Road.

2.5 miles:
Hopewell

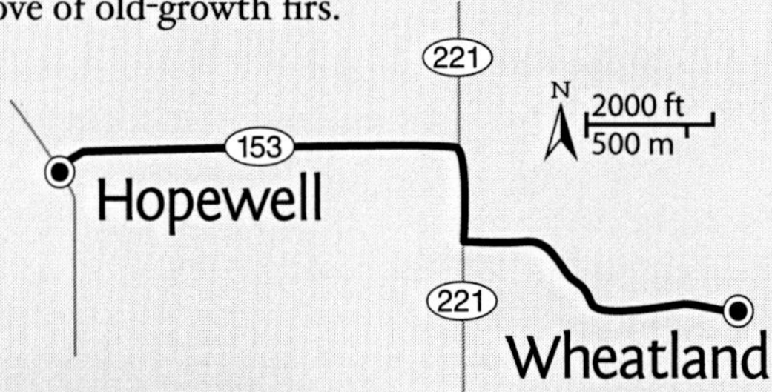

home near Maud Williams State Park

Osprey nest near Wheatland Ferry

Hopewell

Elevation: 178 feet

Location:
45.05.822 N • 123.05.574 W

Services:
food (if store is open), B&B

Nestled in the foothills of the Eola Hills, Hopewell is named for the eager optimism of its early inhabitants. The post office opened in 1897 and closed in 1903. At one time Hopewell had a blacksmith shop, garage, boarding house, and two stores.

Points of Interest

- **Hopewell School**
  (22219 Hopewell Road)
  Opened in 1915 and served students into the 1950s. A school yard swing remains in the front yard of this converted residence.

- **Hopewell Bed and Breakfast**
  (22350 Hopewell Road)
  An old farmhouse that has been remodeled and recently opened as a Bed and Breakfast.

- **Hopewell Store**
  (22262 Hopewell Road)
  Built in 1910.

- **Hopewell Seventh Day Adventist Church**
  Circa 1908.

- **Hopewell Church and Cemetery** *(0.3 miles north on the Lafayette Highway. Turn left onto Church Road)*
  The oldest headstone is dated 1848. Daniel Matheny is buried here.

Hopewell Store

Hopewell to Spring Valley (Zena)

Distance:
7.4 miles

Directions:
Continue traveling west on Hopewell Road.

Points En Route

(mileage from Hopewell Store)

0.4 miles:
1899 Fred Williamson Century Farm. (2340 Hopewell Road).

1.5 miles:
Entering Polk County.

2.6 miles:
Century-old farmhouse.

2.7 miles:
Stangeland Vineyards. Tasting room, panoramic valley views.

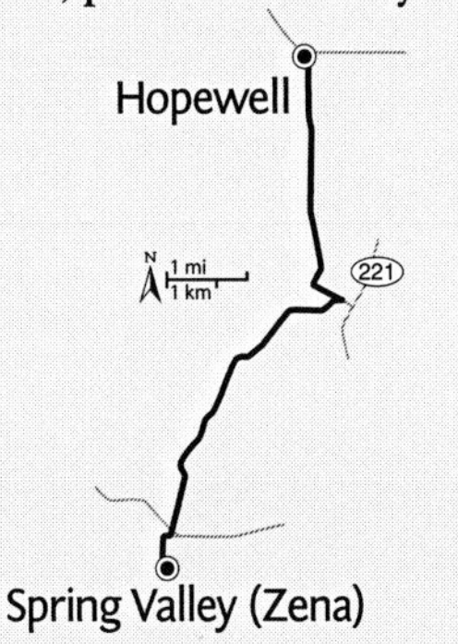

3.1 miles:
Intersection with Spring Valley Road. Turn right.

3.8 miles:
Spring Valley Community Center and Garden Club. Turn left on Bethel Heights Road.

4.9 miles:
Old two-story farm home.

5.4 miles:
Witness Tree Vineyard and tasting room. Named for the old tree that grows on the hill above the tasting room, and that was used as a surveyor's landmark in 1854.

5.7 miles:
Cristom Vineyard, Wine Tasting.

7.0 miles:
Intersection with Zena Road. Continue across Zena Road to Brush College Road.

7.1 miles:
Brush College Road, turn right.

7.4 miles:
Spring Valley (Zena)

Spring Valley (Zena)

Elevation: 231 feet

Location:
45.00.768 N • 123.07.712 W

Services:
none

In the 1840s this area was called Spring Valley due to the large number of naturally occurring fresh water springs. Spring Valley post office opened in 1852 and closed in 1855. In 1863 the Cooper brothers built a store, purchased rights to the post office in 1869, and changed the name of the community to Zena, honoring their wives, Arvazena and Melzena.

Zena Church

Points of Interest

- **Zena Church and Cemetery** Presbyterian Church erected in 1859. The church bell was shipped from England around Cape Horn. The building has a unique rock foundation. An old organ, pews, and many historical photos furnish the sanctuary.

Witness Tree Vineyards

Spring Valley (Zena) to Bethel

Distance:
4.2 miles

Directions:
From the Church and Cemetery turn right onto Brush College Road and return to Zena Road.

Points En Route

(mileage from the Zena Church entrance)

0.1 miles:
Intersection with Zena Road. Turn left.

1.0 miles:
Bryn Mawr Vineyard (turn right to visit the winery).

1.4 miles:
Pioneer Vineyard.

3.1 miles:
Old, two-story farmhouse.

3.7 miles:
Cherry Hill Winery (turn left to visit the tasting room).

4.2 miles:
Turn right into Bethel Church and Bethel College.

4.2 miles:
Bethel

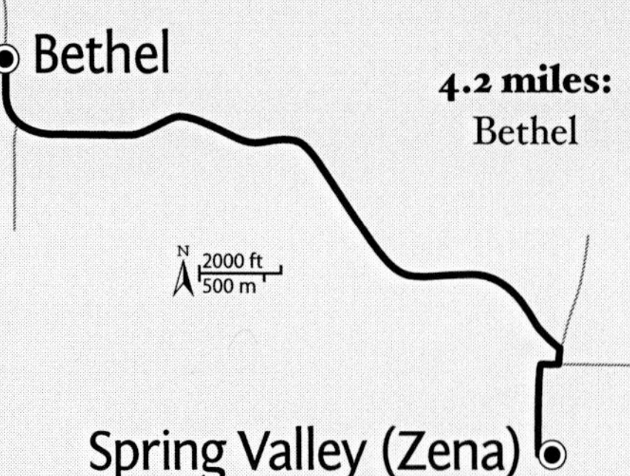

Bethel

Elevation: 216 feet

Location:
45.02.503 N • 123.11.068 W

Services:
none

Located in Plum Valley, Bethel was named in 1846 for a Hebrew word that means 'God's House' or 'Oath of God.' Bethel College was founded in 1855 but discontinued in 1862. The buildings have been used as both a public school and a church. Bethel College is still owned by the Bethel College Board of Trustees.

Bethel College

Points of Interest

- **Bethel College and Church**
  Location for numerous weddings.

road from Bethel to Oak Grove

Bethel to Oak Grove

Distance:
4.9 miles

Directions:
From Bethel School entrance, turn left onto Zena Road and backtrack to Oak Grove Road.

Points En Route

(mileage from Bethel College)

1.0 miles:
Old farmhouse.

1.9 miles:
Frizell Road. Continue on Oak Grove Road.

2.5 miles:
Large hay barn.

3.8 miles:
Pavement returns.

4.3 miles:
Intersection with Crowley Road. Look for the Oak Grove Winery. Stay on Oak Grove Road.

4.6 miles:
Eola Springs Winery to the left. Stay on Oak Grove Road.

4.9 miles:
Oak Grove

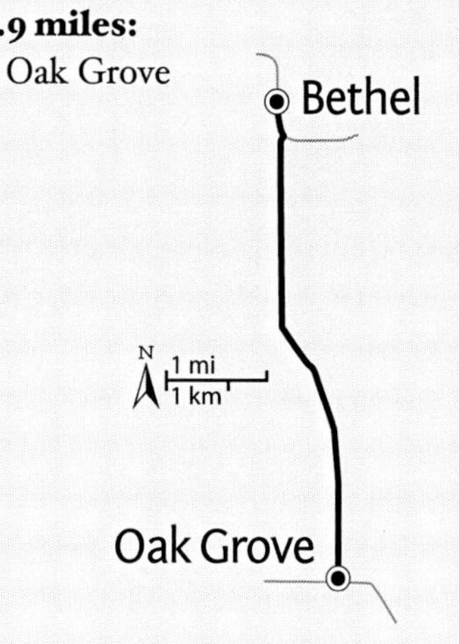

Oak Grove

Elevation: 335 feet

Location:
44.55.759 N • 123.13.679 W

Services:
none

The community was named for the stands of oak trees that grow in the vicinity. Little remains of this Polk County community.

Points of Interest

- **Oak Grove Church**
  Constructed in 1882.

- **Oak Grove School**
  Built in the 1920s and now vacant.

- **Oak Grove Grange #198**
  (adjacent to the school)
  A longtime center for the farming community. Note the 'boot and shoe cleaner' located at the front entrance.

Oak Grove Church

Oak Grove to Rickreall

Distance:
7.6 miles

Directions:
Continue south on Oak Grove Road.

Points En Route

(mileage from Oak Grove Church)

0.1 miles:
Turn left onto Oak Grove Road.

0.8 miles:
Orchard Heights Winery.

3.2 miles:
Intersection with Highway 22. Turn right.
Prepare to turn left in 1.4 miles.

4.6 miles:
Turn left on Greenwood Road.

4.9 miles:
Intersection with Rickreall Road. Site of Greenwood, named for the many trees that grew along the creek. The old Greenwood School building stands near Rickreall Creek, now home to the Polk County HO model railroad club. Turn right and drive west toward Rickreall.

6.5 miles:
Derry, named by James Nesmith after a town in New Hampshire. This small community grew around the railroad that came through in 1912.

6.8 miles:
Three-story barn.

7.6 miles:
Rickreall

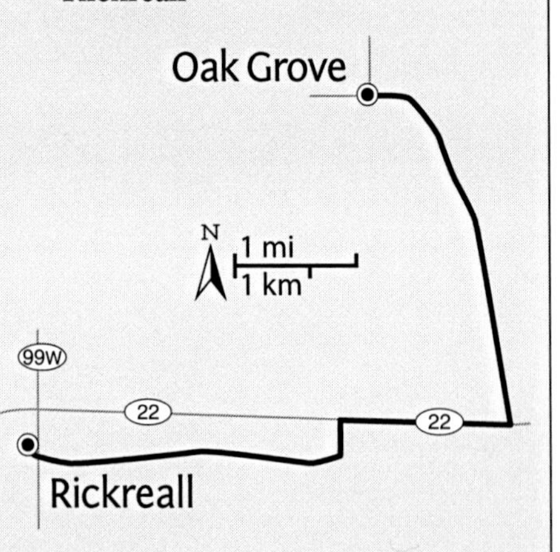

Rickreall

Elevation: 223 feet

Location:
44.55.759 N • 123.13.679 W

Services:
gas, food

Rickreall is Chinook jargon for 'swift water,' and 1830s French trappers may have influenced the pronunciation. The Rickreall post office opened in 1851, closed in 1857, and reopened in 1866. During the Civil War, Rickreall was nicknamed 'Little Dixie' because of the many Southerners in the area.

Rickreall School

Points of Interest

- **Rickreall Grange # 671**
  Located next to the grade school, the grange hall also served as the school gymnasium.
- **Rickreall School**
  Built in 1902, the building now houses the Jubilee Christian Academy.

Rickreall to Monmouth

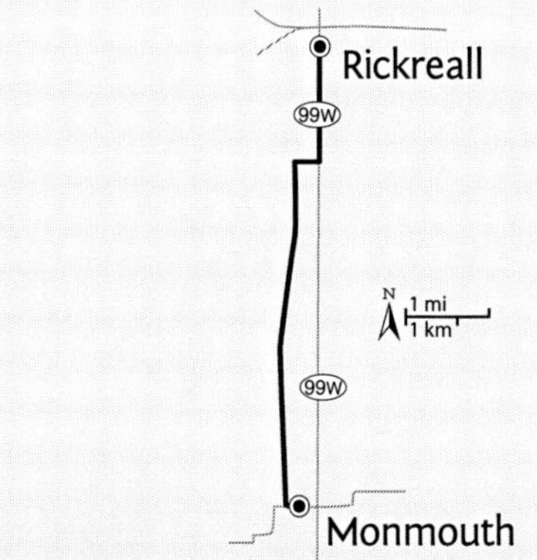

Distance:
5.2 miles

Directions:
At Rickreall Rd and HW 99, turn left toward Monmouth.

Points En Route

(mileage from the stop light)

0.1 miles:
Crossing Rickreall Creek.

0.1 miles:
Eola Hills Winery, tasting room.

0.1 miles:
Polk County Museum and Historical Society.

0.2 miles:
Entrance to Polk County Fairgrounds and Nesmith Park. The park is named for pioneer resident James Nesmith, born in 1820. Nesmith came to Oregon in 1843 and filed a land claim near Monmouth in 1844. In 1845, Nesmith played a major role in forming Oregon's provisional government. He was elected to the territorial legislature in 1847 and helped form Polk County. In 1853 he was appointed US Marshall for the Oregon Territory and was the Superintendent of Indian Affairs from 1857 until 1859. He served as US Senator from 1861 until 1867, and later as US Representative to congress. He is buried in a family plot near the creek, accessed by a trail in the park. His home in Derry was constructed on the on the east side of Rickreall Creek.

1.0 miles:
Turn left on Orrs Corner Road.

1.3 miles:
Turn left on Riddle Road. Poplar tree farm. The trees are grown commercially to make paper.

2.2. miles:
Intersection with Clow Corner Road. Stay on Riddle Road.

5.2 miles:
Monmouth

Monmouth

Elevation: 201 feet

Location:
44.50.911 N • 123.14.122 W

Services:
gas, food, lodging, B&B

Campbell Hall, Western Oregon University

In 1853 pioneers from Monmouth, Illinois settled in the area, filing a 640-Acre land claim to establish a town and a college under the auspices of the Christian Church. Monmouth was platted in 1855. In 1856 the college was surveyed, and a mercantile store opened. The first house was erected in 1857. By 1858 the town had 21 families, a grocery store, cooper, drug store, tavern, harness shop, two blacksmith shops, two wagon makers, and three dry good stores. The post office opened in 1859, two weeks after Oregon became a state. Most of the early buildings were lost to fire. Monmouth was the last remaining "dry town" in the state, losing that status in 2002.

Points of Interest

- **Historical Marker**
  (Main and Knox)
  A sign indicates where the city began in 1856.

- **Monmouth City Park**
  (Main and Warren)
  Picnic, playground, restrooms and an old fountain.

- **Old House** *(212 Knox)*
  1891 construction.

- **Polk County State Bank**
  (Main and Broad)
  The bank was constructed in 1896, using the vault from the bank that burned in 1889.

- **Western Oregon University**
  The school opened as Monmouth University in 1856 and was renamed several times, the last in 1997 as Western Oregon University. The oldest building on campus is Campbell Hall, 1871. Todd Hall was constructed in 1912, Maple Hall in 1913, and the Cottage in 1917.

- **Monmouth Improvement Company Building**
  (105-113 E Main)
  Built in 1902 by a home-owned development company with more than 50,000 locally made bricks.

- **First National Bank** *(193 E Main)*
  Built in 1922.

- **Odd Fellows Hall** *(205 E Main)*
  Erected in 1922. Now houses various downtown businesses.

Odd Fellows Hall

- **Craven House** *(858 E. Main)*
  There is some debate over the age, but most agree it is one of the oldest in Monmouth, and likely constructed around 1869.

- **Evangelical United Brethren Church** *(191 N Monmouth)*
  Built in 1892 and moved to its current location in 1922.

- **First Christian Church** *(189 S Monmouth)*
  Dates to 1877. The old church once stood at the present site of Western Oregon University's Campbell Hall.

- **Thomas Gentle House** *(855 N Monmouth)*
  Now a part of the WOU campus, this home was a private residence in 1880.

- **Old House** *(287 S Monmouth)*
  A bungalow, built in 1890.

- **Hiebert House** *(342 N Monmouth)*
  Dates to 1895.

- **Jensen Arctic Museum** *(590 W Church)*
  The only museum on the west coast devoted to the Arctic Culture. Named for its founder Paul Jensen, former WOU professor.

- **Riley Lane House** *(North of Alberta)*
  Dates to 1880.

- **Historic House** *(391 Jackson)*
  Built in 1892.

- **Monmouth (Fircrest) Cemetery**
  Go south on Knox to Helmick Highway, 2.9 miles. Dates to 1860.

First National Bank

Monmouth to Independence

Distance:
0.8 miles
These two communities have grown together and share a common boundary. The high school was named Central because of its location between the two communities.

Directions:
From Monmouth, drive east on Main.

Points En Route

(mileage from the stop light at Main and Pacific Highway "HW 99W")

0.6 miles:
Skate Park, Little League sports fields, and miniature golf.

0.8 miles:
Independence

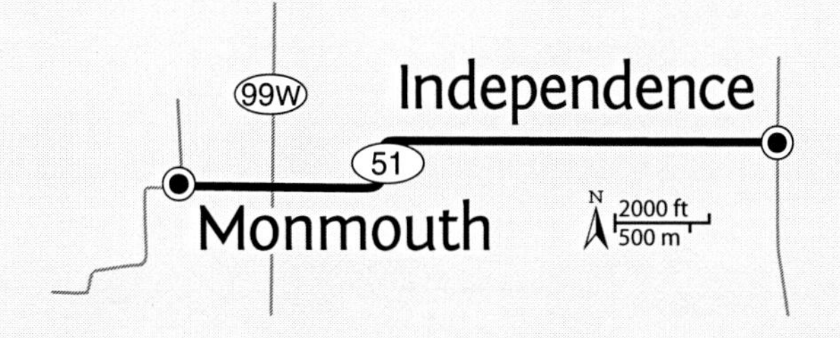

Independence

Elevation: 167 feet

Location:
45.51.119 N • 123.11.294 W

Services:
gas, food, lodging

Independence City Bank

James Thorp, who settled on the east side of Ash Creek, founded Independence in 1845. Thorp platted the town near an Indian burial ground and named it after his hometown in Missouri. The first business here was a saloon at the corner of Grand and Marsh that was also used as a church and a schoolhouse. Henry Hill arrived in 1847 and developed land on the west side of Ash Creek. First competing with Thorp's settlement but then joining it, the two communities officially became one city in 1885. The railroad came to town in 1886, and Independence was linked to neighboring Monmouth by rail in 1890. In the 1930s, Independence was known as the "Hop Capital of the World."

Points of Interest

- **Independence City Bank** *(Main and Monmouth)*
  Constructed in 1889 and since restored to its original condition.

- **Taylor's Drug Store** *(Main and Monmouth)*
  After more than sixty years in business, the venerable drug store and old time soda fountain closed in October of 2006.

- **J.R. Cooper House** *(414 Main)*
  Built in 1910 with leaded glass windows.

- **Henry Hill House** *(614 Main)*
  Constructed in 1870.

- **G.N. Sloper House** *(16 Log Cabin)*
  In Thorps town; built in 1912.

- **Old Christian Church** *(350 A)*
  Dates to 1886. This is where Thorp's town and Hill's town combined into one community.

- **Hodgins-Klosterman House** *(284 B)*
  1885 construction.

- **Riverview Park** *(between B and C, downtown)*
  The park is located on property that was once the home of the "Hop Bowl," where annual hop festivals took place, as well as the site where steamboats and ferries once docked. The park has a boat launch, picnic area, restrooms, amphitheater, and playground.

- **Williams House** *(264 C)*
  Built in 1914.

- **B.F. Whiteaker House** *(363 C)*
  Built in 1891.

Riverview Park amphitheater

- **L.L. Whiteaker House** *(389 C)*
  Built in 1890.

- **C. Ruef House** *(413 C)*
  This home was built in 1890.

- **Independence Depot** *(163 D)*
  The old train depot was built in 1920.

- **Sida Walker House** *(58 2nd)*
  1899 home to a hop farmer.

- **Kirkland House** *(116 2nd)*
  Constructed in 1900.

- **Smith-Gibson House** *(41 3rd)*
  Built in 1880.

- **Independence Heritage Museum** *(112 3rd)*
  The museum's building was formerly the First Baptist Church, built in 1888.

- **Walker House** *(224 3rd)*
  1909 construction.

J.R. Cooper Building

- **Methodist Church Parsonage**
  (260 3rd)
  Built in 1904.

- **Old Methodist Church**
  (290 3rd)
  The first church in Independence.

- **Presbyterian Church**
  (4th and D)
  This is the new church, built in 1927. The old one, built in 1882, was moved to 340 3rd Street and is now home to the Independence Women's Club.

- **Henry Mott House** *(88 4th)*
  This home was built in 1902.

- **Henry Hill Park and Pool**
  (5th and I)
  Named for one of the town founders. The pool opened in the early 1950s.

- **George Skinner House**
  (275 Monmouth)
  Skinner was a steamboat captain.

- **Old Public Library**
  (311 Monmouth)
  Built in 1929. Now a satellite branch to the new library located at 75 Monmouth.

- **W. Craven House**
  (363 Monmouth)
  Built in 1895.

- **J.A. Wheeler House**
  (386 Monmouth)
  Built in 1880.

- **Dr. O.D. Butler House**
  (411 Monmouth)
  Constructed in 1892.

- **Baldwin House** *(461 Monmouth)*
  Occupied in 1895.

- **Vernon J. Brown House**
  (581 Monmouth)
  Built in 1914.

- **Irvine House**
  (593 Monmouth)
  Constructed in 1893.

- **C. Mattson House**
  (615 Monmouth)
  Built in 1895.

- **Pioneer City Park**
  (7th and C)
  Picnic area, restrooms. Ash Creek runs through the park.

- **Eldridge House**
  (7th and Monmouth)
  Built in 1914. Eldridge owned and operated the Independence Creamery.

- **Mountain Fir Lumber Company** *(8th and F)*
  Big part of the local economy for many years.

- **Hilltop Cemetery**
  (south of town on Corvallis Road)
  Dates to the 1870s.

Henry Hill House

Independence to Buena Vista

Distance:
7.0 miles

Directions:
From the corner of Main and Monmouth, go south.

Points En Route

(mileage from the old bank)

1.4 miles:
Turn left on Buena Vista Road.

1.4 miles:
Descend into the fertile bottomlands.

2.9 miles:
Old farm, barn, and outbuildings.

3.9 miles:
Turn right on Buena Vista Road.

6.3 miles:
Old three-story home.

7.0 miles:
Buena Vista

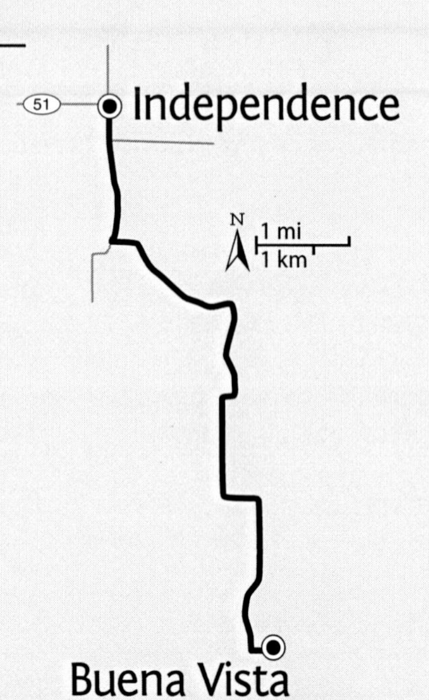

bottomlands near Buena Vista

Buena Vista

Elevation: 172 feet

Location:
44.46.216 N • 123.05.869 W

Services:
food, B&B (when open)

Buena Vista Ferry Landing

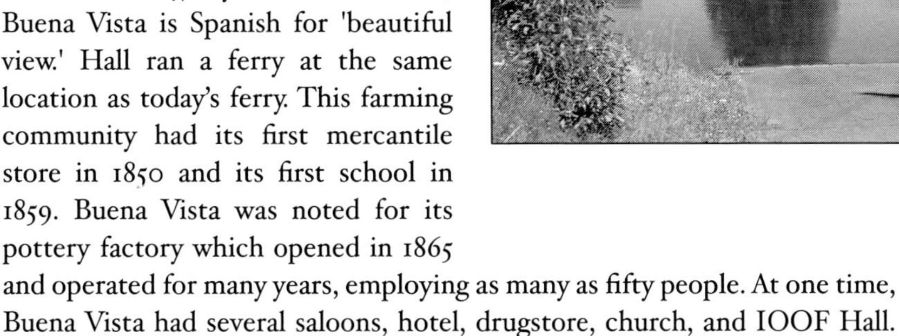

Settled in 1847 by Reason B. Hall, Buena Vista is Spanish for 'beautiful view.' Hall ran a ferry at the same location as today's ferry. This farming community had its first mercantile store in 1850 and its first school in 1859. Buena Vista was noted for its pottery factory which opened in 1865 and operated for many years, employing as many as fifty people. At one time, Buena Vista had several saloons, hotel, drugstore, church, and IOOF Hall. Buena Vista was a national leader in hop production until the 1950s and was once considered as a site for the state capitol. The railroad bypassed the town, leading to its decline.

Points of Interest

- **Buena Vista Ferry**
  (on Willamette Ferry Street)
  Buena Vista got its first modern ferry from Independence in 1950, the year the bridge over the Willamette was completed. Osprey frequently nest on a pole located on the east side ferry landing.

- **Buena Vista County Park**
  (on Park Street near the ferry landing)
  Boat launch, picnic area, and primitive toilets.

- **Buena Vista School**
  (11305 Meridian)
  Now a private residence, the school was built in 1902.

- **Buena Vista Church**
  (Main and Church)
  The old church still has its bell.

- **Buena Vista House**
  (Sequoia and Riverview)
  Café and lodging. Open occasionally.

- **Hilltop Cemetery**
  Dates to the 1850s, it is also known as the IOOF Cemetery.

Buena Vista B&B

Buena Vista House

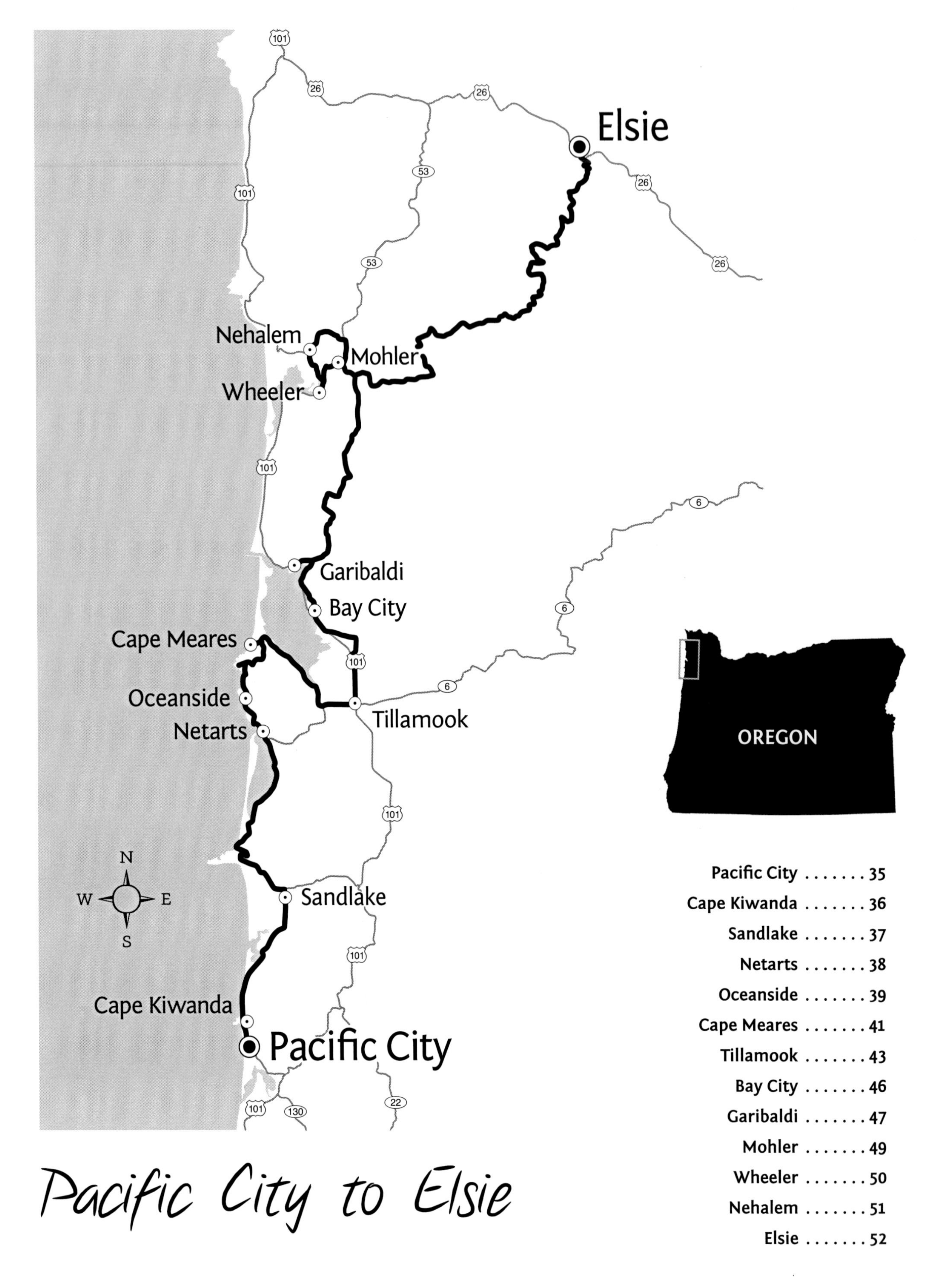

Pacific City to Elsie

Exploring Three Capes – Kiwanda, Meares and Lookout

Pacific City to Elsie (89 miles)

This route begins at Pacific City and progresses to Cape Kiwanda State Park and Natural Area at the north end of the community. The road meanders north, following a rugged coastline that provides ocean vistas, wildlife viewing, and hiking trails.

The three capes – Kiwanda, Meares, and Lookout – are reminders of nature's erosive power. Bring binoculars for bird watching and cameras for picture taking. Potential activities for the traveler on this coastal route include antiquing, wine tasting, touring a cheese factory and a blimp hangar, fishing, riding dune buggies, camping, picnicking and tide pooling. Remember to bring a jacket; the weather is unpredictable and changes at a moments notice.

Three Arch Rocks at Oceanside

Pacific City

Elevation: 22 feet

Location:
45.12.901 N • 123.57.382 W

Services:
gas, food, lodging, camping, RV, B&B

Pacific City is named because of its closeness to the Pacific Ocean. Platted under the name of Ocean Park in 1893, the name changed to Pacific City when the post office opened in 1909. The first school in Pacific City opened in 1910. The downtown borders the Nestucca River rather than the ocean. The town has gradually spread toward the sea and the Cape Kiwanda area is the present population hub. The Killamooks and Nestugga Indians were the first peoples in the area, with whites settling here in the 1870s.

Points of Interest

- **Nestucca Bay** *(Brooten Road follows the river on the way to town)* This estuary and its wetlands are home to many species of birds and wildlife. Many people try their luck at salmon and steelhead fishing in these waters.

Haystack Rock

Cape Kiwanda

Cape Kiwanda

Elevation: 229 feet (atop the dunes)

Location:
45.13.149 N • 123.58.472 W
(located at the northern end of Pacific City)

Services:
gas, food, lodging, camping, RV, B&B

Cape Kiwanda, originally known as Sand Cape, was named for the nearby mountains of sand. It is the smallest of the three capes on this trip, rising several hundred feet above the ocean. Haystack Rock, which reaches a height of 327 feet and lies about a mile off Cape Kiwanda, is a highly eroded sandstone escarpment that is extremely susceptible to the changing coastal weather. It is thought that Haystack Rock and the cape are of the same land formation, which extends almost one mile under the Pacific Ocean. The cape received its name from the chief of the local Nestucca Indians, Kiwanda. Near the cape are mountains of sand, with its dunes among the most climbed on the Oregon Coast. The dory fleet – a dory is a lightweight fishing boat, approximately 15-22 feet in length, characterized by a flat bottom whose fore and aft are angled at about 30 degrees – launches from the base of the sand and cape. Whales are frequently spotted less than one-quarter mile offshore in front of Haystack Rock. Hang gliders launch from the dunes, and wind surfers frequent the calmer, somewhat protected waters nearby. The area is one of the most photographed on the Oregon Coast.

Points of Interest

- **Cape Kiwanda Natural Area**
  (north end of Pacific City on McPhillips Drive)
  Hike, climb, picnic, swim, windsurf. The park area extends more than six miles from the cape, almost touching the community of Sandlake to the north.

- **Haystack Rock**
  This famous monolith stands 327 feet tall, almost 100-feet higher than it other coastal namesake, located at Cannon Beach. (Three geologic features share this name; the second near Cannon Beach and the third in Wallowa County) Home to numerous seabirds, Haystack Rock is basalt that has resisted millennia of erosion.

- **Dory Launching**
  Anglers launch their dories into the surf to fish the rich offshore grounds.

- **Whale Watching**
  Whales frequent the areas around Cape Kiwanda and Haystack Rock.

Cape Kiwanda to Sandlake

Distance:
6.8 miles

Directions:
Travel north on McPhillips Drive.

Points En Route

(mileage from the parking lot on McPhillips Drive across from the Inn at Cape Kiwanda)

1.4 miles:
Intersection with Ferry Road. Continue on McPhillips, heading north.

2.2 miles:
Tierra Del Mar. This small community, originally named by Spanish mariners, means "land of the sea." Many vacation homes.

2.6 miles:
Pier Avenue Rock Shop.

3.8 miles:
Whalen Island RV Park.

4.2 miles:
Clay Myers State Natural Area (Whalen Island).

6.8 miles:
Sandlake

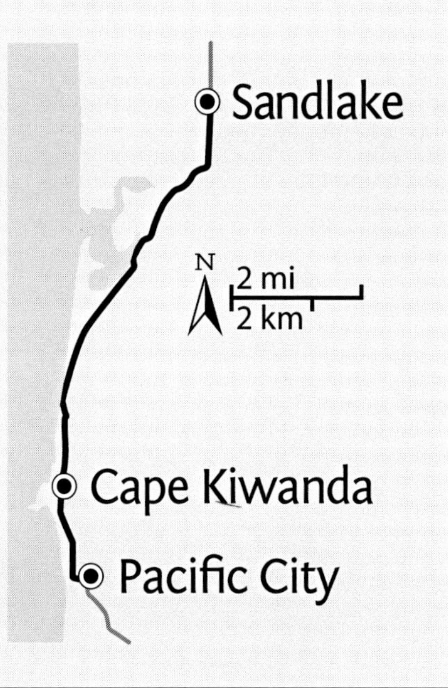

Sandlake

Elevation: 47 feet

Location:
45.18.215 N • 123.55.393 W

Services:
food, gas, camping, B&B

Sandlake got its start as Hembree in 1890, when the first post office opened. In 1898 the name was changed to Sandlake – Sand Lake is also used in the area – for the estuary where it is situated.

Points of Interest

- **Sand Lake**
  The large, seawater estuary.
- **Sand Lake Store** *(corner of Galloway and Sand Lake Road)*
  The old store was constructed in the early 1900s.
- **Nestucca Fire and Rescue** *(across the street from the store)*
  Locals say that the paramedics here work overtime in the summer due to numerous OHV accidents that occur on the dunes.
- **Sand Lake State Park** *(2.3 miles west of the store on Galloway)*
  The park has almost 200 camping sites as well as picnicking, fishing, and bird watching. OHV permits are required for Memorial Day, Fourth of July and Labor Day weekends.

Sandlake to Netarts

Distance:
12.3 miles

Directions:
From the Sand Lake Store, turn left on Sand Lake Road and drive north.

Points En Route

(mileage from the intersection of Galloway and Sand Lake Roads)

1.0 miles:
Intersection. Turn left on Cape Lookout Road.

1.7 miles:
Small pine trees and much sand.

1.9 miles:
The Watershed Interpretive marker.

2.3 miles:
Meriwether Boy Scout Camp.

3.8 miles:
Cape Lookout State Park. Cape Lookout, which rises more than 400 feet above sea level, is the second of the three capes along this route. The highway meanders through the park. Many campsites, including yurts and cabins, and more than eight miles of hiking trails. Until the 1850s, Cape Lookout was actually named Cape Meares.

4.2 miles:
Cape Lookout Trail Head. Down the trail is the site where a WWII bomber crashed.

5.7 miles:
View of Netarts Bay.

7.0 miles:
State Park camping entrance.

9.4 miles:
Whiskey Creek Fish Hatchery.

9.9 miles:
Whiskey Creek Café.

10.9 miles:
Turn left on Netarts Bay Road.

11.7 miles:
Netarts Bay RV Park and Marina.

12.3 miles:
Netarts

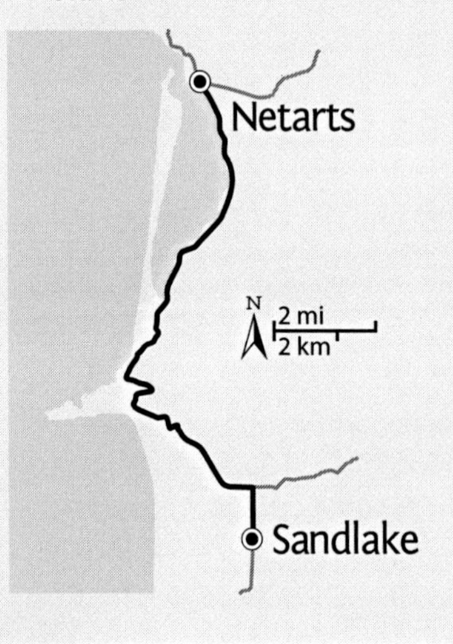

ATVs at Sand Lake State Park

Netarts

Elevation: 40 feet

Location:
45.27.605 N • 123.58.172 W

Services:
gas, food, lodging, RV Park

A year-round population of more than 700 residents live near the bay, protected from wind and waves by the Netarts Sand Spit. Netarts is a Killamook Indian word, meaning 'by the water.' In 1855, a government surveyor parceled the land, and in 1856 Warren Vaught established the first land-grant claim. Beginning in the 1860s, tons of oysters were shipped to San Francisco, with over-harvesting depleting most of the natural beds. The first homes were constructed in 1863 and the post office opened in 1871. The first school was constructed in 1880 and the cemetery had its first burial in 1889 when Abraham McCormick died. The first saw mill was built in the 1890s, the first store opened in 1906, and in 1911 the railroad connected Tillamook to Netarts.

Points of Interest

- **Netarts Interpretive Area**
  (Netarts Boat Basin Road)
  Kiosk with information about the watershed. Boat launch and primitive restrooms.

view from Cape Lookout

Netarts Bay

Netarts to Oceanside

Distance:
2.3 miles

Directions:
From the intersection of Highway 131 and Netarts Bay Road, continue north on Highway 131.

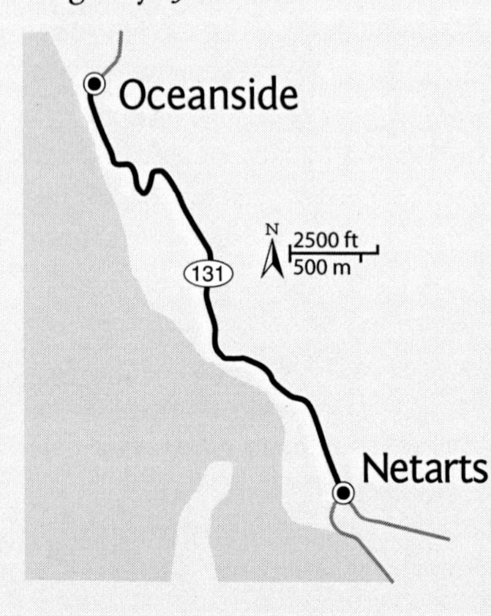

Points En Route

(mileage from the intersection of Highway 131 and Netarts Bay Road)

This route is called the "Three Capes Scenic Loop."

0.8 miles:
Happy Camp, once a logging settlement. The original community was wiped out by a tidal wave in 1896.

2.3 miles:
Oceanside

Oceanside

Oceanside

Elevation: Sea level to 200 feet

Location:
45.27.605 N • 123.58.172 W

Services:
gas, food, lodging

Built diagonally on the side of a rocky incline, Oceanside is named for its location next to the sea. Oceanside was first settled in 1885 by John Maxwell, and is now home to a year-round population of more than 300 as well as many weekend "cottages."

Points of Interest

- **Oceanside Recreation Site**
  (near intersection of Pacific and Maxwell)
  Picnic area and restroom, and beach access.

- **Three Arch Rocks National Wildlife Refuge**
  (400 yards offshore from the Oceanside Recreation Site)
  This was the first wildlife refuge west of the Mississippi River, designated in 1907. It covers more than fifteen acres and is the seasonal home to more than 230,000 seabirds, including common murres, tufted puffins, and storm petrels. It is also a pupping site for the Stellar Sea Lions.

- **Lost Boy Cave**
  (middle of Three Arch Rocks)
  In the base one of the middle rock of the three that form the Arch Rocks is a cave, accessible only by boat. It was named for a young boy who perished as he tried to take refuge there during an incoming storm.

- **Agate Beach**
  (North of the Oceanside Picnic area)
  At low tide, rock hounds can collect agates.

Oceanside to Cape Meares

Distance:
3.6 miles

Directions:
From Pacific Avenue and Highway 131, turn left and drive north.

Points En Route

(mileage from the intersection of Highway 131 and Pacific Avenue)

Highway 131 becomes Cape Meares Loop Road at Pacific Ave.

0.9 miles:
Dramatic view of the Pacific and Cape Meares.

1.1 miles:
Intersection with Radar Road. Continue on Cape Meares Loop Road. (stretches of rough road)

1.6 miles:
Rock Quarry.

2.4 miles:
Turn left on Lighthouse Road; proceed to state Park.

2.5 miles:
Cape Meares State Scenic Viewpoint and National Wildlife Refuge.

Points of Interest at the Viewpoint:

- **Cape Meares State Park**
This park, established in 1938, offers picnicking, hiking, and educational kiosks. Bring binoculars to view the peregrine falcons, nearly extinct in the 1970s, that nest on the cliff a short distance from the lighthouse. Cape Meares is home to a variety of birds, as well as sea and land mammals. Over 250,000 common murres reside here.

- **Cape Meares Lighthouse**
Commissioned in 1890, this is the shortest of Oregon's Lighthouses, standing only thirty-eight feet in height, yet its beacon was once visible for more than twenty miles. The light is projected through an eight-sided lens, one of only two in the United States. It was decommissioned in 1963, then fell to decay and vandalism until restored by "Friends of the Cape Meares Lighthouse."

- **Octopus Tree**
(on the hill above the park)
This sixty-foot diameter Sitka Spruce (*Picea sitchensis*) was once a burial tree shaped to hold the canoes. Referred to by Native Americans as the Council Tree, it may be one of the oldest trees in Oregon.

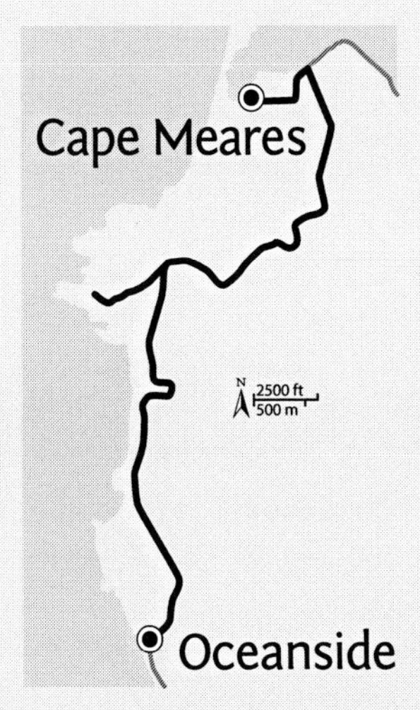

- **Pillar Rock**
(in the ocean, west of the lighthouse)
This large rock is home to numerous seabirds.

(From the park, return to Cape Meares Loop Road and turn left. Add 2.5 miles to mileage)

3.0 miles:
Rough road and a slide area.

3.5 miles:
Turn left on Bayocean Road and drive toward the community of Cape Meares.

3.6 miles:
Cape Meares

Cape Meares State Park

Cape Meares Lighthouse

Cape Meares

Elevation: 82 feet

Location:
45.29.931 N • 123.57.519 W

Services:
none

Cape Meares was named in 1788 to honor John Meares, an early English lieutenant in the British Navy, who sailed along this part of the coast. While on his expedition he named Cape Lookout. Meares called the Arch Rocks the 'Three Brothers' and wrote about the abundant bird life on these giant rock formations. Meares was the first white man to sail into Tillamook Bay. Today, the community of Cape Meares, north of the state scenic area, is a unique blend of old and new homes.

former Cape Meares School

Points of Interest

- **Cape Meares School**
  No longer used as a school, the building retains its original flavor and serves as the community center.

Bayocean Spit

Cape Meares to Tillamook

Distance:
6.5 miles

Directions:
Return to Cape Meares Loop Road, turn left, and travel north to Tillamook on Bayocean Road

Points En Route

(mileage from the intersection of Bayocean Road and Cape Meares Loop Road)

0.1 miles:
Bayocean Boat Launch.

0.3 miles:
Historical Marker. Site of Bayocean, a once large community established in 1906 by real estate investor and land speculator T.B. Potter. Potter hoped to create a second Atlantic City on the Oregon Coast. Frances B. Mitchell bought the first lot in the new development in 1907 and was the last to leave in 1952. By 1912, a post office, a general store, a three-story hotel, a bowling alley, a tin shop, and a bakery were operational. The hotel was fancy for its time, having automatic fire sprinklers and a huge natatorium with a 50 by 160 feet swimming pool. Over four miles of city pavement connected the community's streets, complete with electric light posts, city water, telephones and narrow gauge railroad. By 1914 more than 600 building lots had been sold, involving over 2,000 people. Poorly situated on sinking and unstable ground, the natatorium had eroded away by 1934, with twenty homes falling into the sea by 1949. Storms continued to damage the community, and in 1952 it became an island, separated from the mainland. In the late 1950s, the last remaining homes were moved to high ground, leaving only memories of the community's existence. A one-way drive along Bayocean Spit takes the traveler over the land that once held the community. Today more than 200 species of birds flourish in this estuary.

0.7 miles:
The road parallels Tillamook Bay.

2.1 miles:
Old pilings, the site of a fish cannery.

2.9 miles:
More pilings.

3.9 miles:
Boat launch.

4.0 miles:
Oyster Farm.

4.1 miles:
Old home.

4.9 miles:
Dairy farm, one of many in Tillamook County.

5.3 miles:
Intersection with Highway 131. Turn left and drive east.

5.4 miles:
Crossing the Tillamook River.

5.6 miles:
Myrtle Wood factory.

6.3 miles:
Trask River.

6.5 miles:
Tillamook

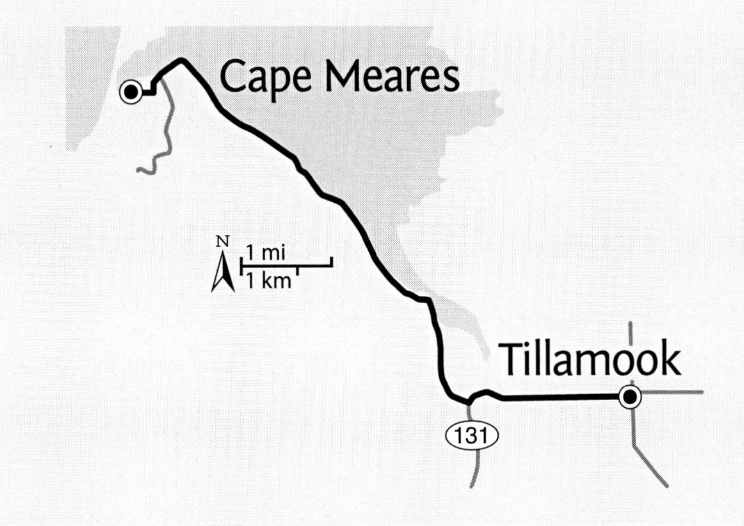

Tillamook

Elevation: 75 feet

Location:
45.27.358 N • 123.50.639 W

Services:
gas, food, lodging, RV, B&B

Tillamook Cheese Factory

The seat of government and county's oldest city, Tillamook is named for the Killamook Tribe who inhabited the area and who are members of the larger Salish group of Native Americans. Tillamook was previously named Lincoln, Hoquarton, the Landing and Tillamook Landing. In 1862, Thomas Stillwell, age seventy-one, opened the first store and platted the town. The post office opened in 1866, seven years after Oregon became a state. In 1873, the first jail was constructed, and Tillamook incorporated in 1891. The telegraph came to town in 1893, paved streets and the railroad in 1911. Tillamook's main industries are dairy farming, cheese making and tourism.

Points of Interest

- **Tillamook Bookstore**
  (218 Pacific Avenue)
  Formerly the Tillamook Apartments and 1912 Tillamook Hotel Annex. Look for the second story hall that connected the apartments and the hotel.

- **Ninth Street Park**
  (9th and Stillwell)
  Tennis courts, picnic area, playground and restrooms.

- **Carnahan Park**
  (west end of 5th Street)
  Picnic, boat launch, restrooms.

- **Dorian's Photography**
  (4th and Main)
  First opened as the livery stable, and later as a radio repair shop.

- **St. Peters Lutheran Church**
  (4th and Madrona)
  Services held here since 1899.

- **Goodspeed Park** *(3rd Street)*
  Basketball court, skateboard area, picnic tables, playground and restrooms.

- **The Pancake House**
  (3rd and Main)
  Built as Ford's Drugstore and Soda Fountain.

- **IOOF Cemetery**
  (off 3rd and Wilson River Loop)
  Dates to the late 1890s.

- **Masonic Lodge** *(2nd and Main)*
  Built in 1914.

- **IOOF Hall** *(2nd and Main)*
  The 1916 lodge is undergoing major remodeling.

Masonic Lodge

- **Tillamook County Museum** *(2106 2nd)*
Housed in the 1905 courthouse, the Pioneer Museum has amassed a huge collection of information about the area and its people. The collection includes scud missile fragments, a violin made from the Octopus tree, pioneer artifacts, and detailed information on the 1933 Tillamook Burn that charred over 355,000 acres. An 1862 millstone that came from the county's first gristmill is located outside the museum.

- **Thayer Bank** (*1802 1st)*
Tillamook's 1895 bank building. The word 'Bank' is located on the building façade.

- **Latimer Quilt and Textile Center** *(2105 Wilson River Loop)*
The old Maple Leaf Schoolhouse houses the living arts center. Opening in 1992, the center showcases regional textiles and touring exhibits. Admission fee.

- **Tillamook Forest Center** *(45500 Wilson River Highway)*
Located in the Tillamook Burn, the center is owned and operated by the Oregon Department of Forestry, helping visitors understand and appreciate our connection with the forests.

- **Trout Cemetery** *(Evergreen and Wilson River Highway)*
A small memorial park.

- **Blue Heron Cheese Company** *(one mile north of downtown on Highway 101)*
A 1930s barn houses the restaurant, gift shop and wine tasting and a petting zoo for children.

- **Tillamook Naval Air Museum** *(6030 Hangar Road- One mile south on Highway 101)*
Opening in 1942 to house K-series dirigibles, the blimp hangar is 192 feet high, nearly 300 feet wide and more than 1,000 feet long. Today it is home to over twenty vintage aircraft including Corsairs, P-51 Mustangs and Messerschmitts. The air museum is one of two similar hangars that were constructed with the second hangar burning in 1992.

- **Tillamook Cheese Factory** *(two miles north on Highway 101)*
Making cheese since 1909, the Tillamook Creamery Association is open for tours. In front of the factory is a replica of the Morning Star, an 1854 ship that transported cheese and dairy products to Portland and Astoria. The first cheese factory was originally located in the community of Juno, north of its present location.

- **Port of Tillamook Bay Railroad**
The Tillamook Bay Railroad offers scenic coastal excursions on a dinner train that runs from Wheeler to Timber and Garibaldi to Wheeler.

Tillamook County Museum

Steam mill outside the museum

Tillamook to Bay City

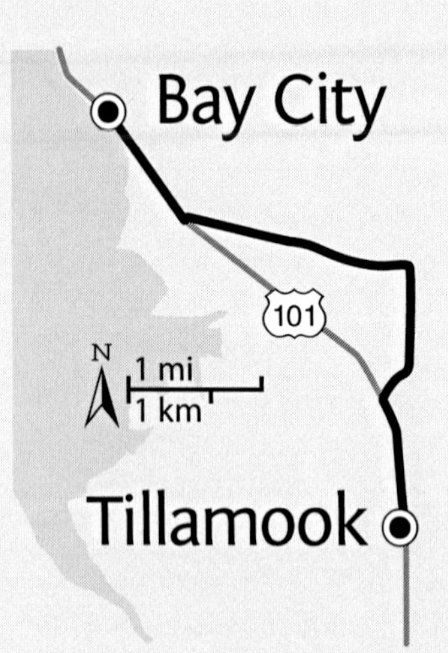

Distance:
4.2 miles

Directions:
From the Tillamook Cheese Factory, go north on Highway 101.

Points En Route

(mileage from the Cheese Factory)

This route is called the "Three Capes Scenic Loop."

0.3 miles:
Juno Hill. The former community of Juno was named for a settler's home in North Carolina, and was site of the first Tillamook Cheese Factory. The community of Juno was located at 45.29.221 N • 123.50.437 W.

0.6 miles:
Alderbrook Loop Road; turn right.

0.8 miles:
Park and boat ramp on the Kilchis River. Five rivers drain into Tillamook Bay: The Kilchis, Tillamook, Trask, Wilson (the longest) and Miami. This, along with heavy rainfall, contributes to frequent flooding.

1.2 miles:
Dairy, one of Tillamook's many.

1.5 miles:
Idaville Grange and the 1922 Idaville schoolhouse (intersection of Kilchis River Road and Alderbrook Road). The Idaville Cemetery is 2.7 miles east on Kilchis River Road.

1.6 miles:
Turn left, staying on Alderbrook Loop Road.

2.1 miles:
Intersection with Doughty Road; stay on Alderbrook.

2.4 miles:
Idaville, platted in 1870 and named for the eldest daughter of Warren Vaughn, one of the area's first settlers.

2.6 miles:
One of the first homes in Idaville.

2.7 miles:
Idaville Grocery and Gas.

3.4 miles:
Junction with Highway 101; turn right onto the highway and drive north.

4.2 miles:
Bay City

Dairy cows near Tillamook

Oyster shells near Bay City

Bay City

Elevation: 68 feet

Location:
45.31.315 N • 123.53.209 W

Services:
gas, food

Bay City has always been considered as the "town down by the bay." The city was incorporated in 1888 and the post office opened in 1889. Interestingly, the community's first postmaster hailed from Bay City, Michigan. A devastating flood in the 1890s wiped-out much of the town. Main Street used to be Highway 101 until the 1950s when it was rerouted. Today, you will find oyster farming on the ocean side of Highway 101 as well as a restaurant and fish market.

Masonic Lodge

Points of Interest

- **United Methodist Church** *(5th and Main)*
  Built in1893 with stained glass windows.

- **Masonic Lodge** *(Main and A)*
  Built in 1927, now an art gallery and site of the first post office and city's first general store.

- **Old House** *(9545 Main)*
  The first house to be constructed after the 1890s flood.

Old House

Bay City to Garibaldi

Distance:
3.6 miles

Directions:
Travel north on Main Street, old highway 101.

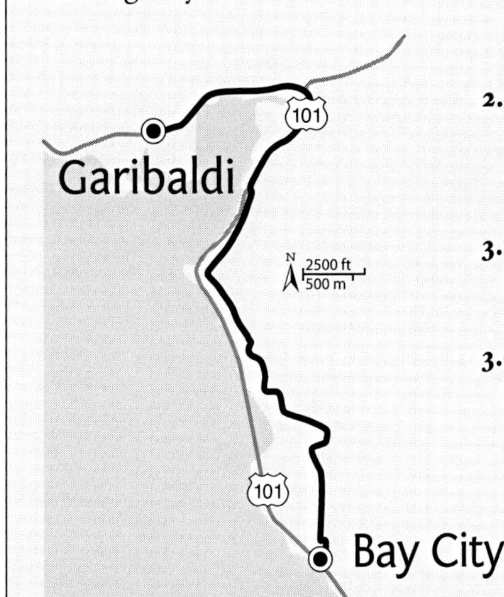

Points En Route

(mileage from the Masonic Lodge/Art Gallery)

0.6 miles:
Stand of old Douglas fir trees.

2.5 miles:
Intersection with Highway 101; turn right and drive north.

3.1 miles:
Cross the Miami River.

3.6 miles:
Garibaldi

Garibaldi

Elevation: 30 feet

Location:
45.33.581 N • 123.54.410 W

Services:
gas, food, lodging, RV parks

Coast Guard Station

Garibaldi is a quaint, coastal community nestled between two mountains. The community is named to honor Italian patriot Giuseppe Garibaldi, who never set foot on the Pacific coast. Joseph Champion was the first settler in Tillamook County, and lived a short time in Garibaldi. The Garibaldi post office opened in 1870, becoming the third in Tillamook County. The community was once dependent upon the timber industry and commercial fishing as its main industries, but now relies on tourism and sport fishing to sustain its economy.

Points of Interest

- **Lumberman's Park**
  (American Avenue)
  Old railroad cars and depot and the world's largest circular saw blade and numerous logging items. There is a playground and picnic area with restrooms in the small park. A unique concrete telephone booth rests on the corner of American and Jerry Creasy Drive. Phone wires still hang from inside the booth and blue, glass insulators sit atop the telephone poles. Railroad excursion tickets may be purchased at the booth. A restored 1910 Heisler locomotive and coach car are adjacent to the depot.

- **Garibaldi RV Park – Old Mill Resort**
  (American and Jerry Creasy)
  In 1977 this RV park was built on the site of a lumber mill. The tall (225 feet) 1927 smokestack stands, as do several of the old mill structures. One old mill building houses a tackle shop.

- **Garibaldi Maritime Museum**
  (112 Garibaldi)
  A sculpture of Captain Robert Gray stands near the entrance to the museum, and a half hull of his ship Columbia Redivida is displayed inside. Admission charge.

- **Old Pharmacy** *(230 Garibaldi)*
  Constructed years ago.

- **Old Grocery** *(234 Garibaldi)*
  Today, an antique store.

- **Garibaldi Hardware Store**
  (301 Garibaldi)
  Constructed in the early 1900s.

- **Garibaldi Bakery** *(302 Garibaldi)*
  Making bread and pastries a long time.

Garibaldi docks

- **Garibaldi Marina**
  (302 Mooring Basin Road)
  Boat launch, restaurants and charter fishing.

- **Antique Store** *(406 Garibaldi)*
  Originally the first drugstore in Garibaldi, it had several apartments on the second floor.

- **Old Baptist Church**
  (410 Garibaldi)
  The first church in Garibaldi.

- **Methodist Church**
  (Garibaldi and 5th)
  Dedicated in 1893 and still in use.

- **Garibaldi School**
  (Cypress and 6th)
  Constructed in 1913; additional classrooms have been added through the years.

- **God's Lighthouse Church**
  (Garibaldi and 8th)
  An early 20th century church building.

- **Coast Guard Station**
  (1200 Garibaldi)
  The two-story facility overlooks the bay.

- **Robert Gray Historical Marker**
  (just north of town on Highway 101)
  Near this point on August of 1788, Gray entered Tillamook Bay.

Garibaldi Depot at Lumberman's Park

Garibaldi to Mohler

Distance:
13.7 miles

Directions:
Back track from downtown and drive east to the Miami River Road.

Points En Route

(mileage from Garibaldi and 1st, the Old Mill RV Park)

0.5 miles:
Miami River Junction sign.

0.6 miles:
Turn left onto Miami River Rd.

2.1 miles:
Intersection with Moss Creek Road. Stay on Miami River Rd.

4.5 miles:
Remains of an old mill and warehouse.

8.1 miles:
Old farmhouse.

8.2 miles:
Crossing Foley Creek.

8.3 miles:
Site of Barnesdale, a community named in 1912 for Frank Barnes, the first postmaster.

10.6 miles:
Site of an old cedar shake mill. "Badminton Bird" burner remains.

12.5 miles:
Railroad tracks.

13.4 miles:
Intersection with Highway 53, turn left traveling toward Tillamook.

13.7 miles:
Mohler

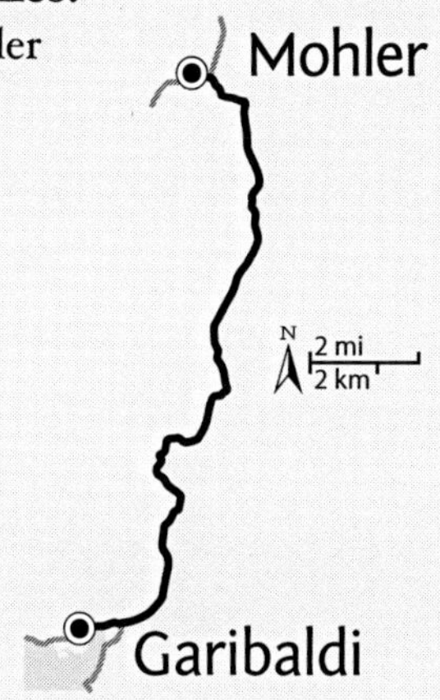

Mohler

Elevation: 48 feet

Location:
42.42.023 N • 123.53.107 W

Services:
gas, food

The post office opened in 1897 under the name of Foley Creek and quickly changed to Balm in the same year. The name was changed to Mohler in 1911, to honor A.L. Mohler, president of the Union Pacific Railroad.

Point of Interest

- **Nehalem Bay Winery**
  (34965 Highway 53)
  Noted for unique costal blends of wine and an annual Blue Grass Festival. The winery is built on the site of the 1907 Zwiefel Creamery. The cheesemaker's home still stands behind the winery. A hotel and railroad once stood nearby.

Nehalem Bay Winery

Mohler to Wheeler

Distance:
1.8 miles

Directions:
From the intersection of Miami River Road and Highway 53, proceed west to Highway 101.

Points En Route

(mileage from the intersection of Miami River Rd and Highway 53)

0.2 miles:
Remains of an old mill.

1.1 miles:
Turn left onto Highway 101.

1.8 miles:
Wheeler

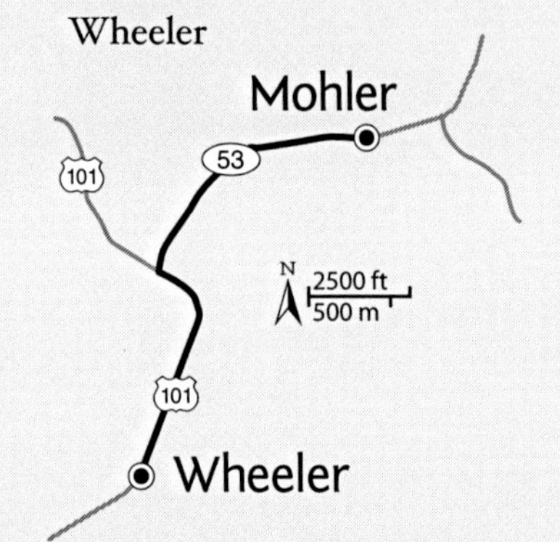

Nehalem Bay off Wheeler

Wheeler

Elevation: 70 feet

Location:
45.41.354 N • 123.52.929 W

Services:
gas, food, lodging

Wheeler Hotel

Wheeler was first settled in 1880 and named for Coleman H. Wheeler, early lumberman and owner of the local sawmill that, at one time, was the largest on the West Coast. The town incorporated in 1914. Wheeler was once home to a bank, a hardware store, two grocery stores, two drug stores, two gas stations, two car dealerships, and several canneries (all that remains of the canneries are the pilings still visible in the river). Until the 1950s, Wheeler was the southern end of Highway 101.

Points of Interest

- **Wheeler Hotel** *(47 Gregory)*
  This business opened in 1920. The old hotel phone, desk, radio and hall tree are located in the lobby. In 1940, the bottom floor became the Rinehart Clinic, a nationally renowned Arthritis clinic. Three generations of Rinehart's ran the office and worked in the hospital.

- **Masonic Lodge**
  (63 Nehalem Blvd)
  Lodge #102 was built circa 1920.

- **Wheeler Liquor Store**
  (327 Nehalem Blvd)
  It was originally Wheeler's first meat market and general store.

- **Plymouth Dealership**
  (393 Nehalem Blvd)
  Opened in 1913. An old Richfield gas pump and island remain.

- **Ford Dealership**
  (425 Nehalem Blvd)
  This facility opened in 1918 and is now an antique store..

- **Wheeler Hardware**
  (445 Nehalem Blvd)
  Open since 1917.

- **Nehalem Post Office**
  A triangular shaped building between Gregory and Rorvik.

- **Livery Stable** *(117 Hall)*
  The owner of the livery stable lived in the top story and conducted business on the lower floor.

- **Old Country Inn**
  (300 Block of Hall)
  Vacant and dilapidated.

- **City Hall** *(corner of Hospital Road and Nehalem)*
  Next to the fire hall.

- **Lower Wheeler Park**
  Restrooms, picnic, and boat launch.

- **Upper Wheeler Park**
  (drive up Hospital Road)
  A small park with a picnic area and playground. No restrooms.

Wheeler to Nehalem

Distance:
1.9 miles

Directions:
Go north on Highway 101.

Points En Route

(mileage from Hwy 101 and Spruce)

0.8 miles:
Intersection with Highway 53. Drive north on Highway 101.

1.3 miles:
Tideland Road. Restrooms and boat launch. Stay on 101.

1.5 miles:
Crossing the Nehalem River.

1.9 miles:
Nehalem

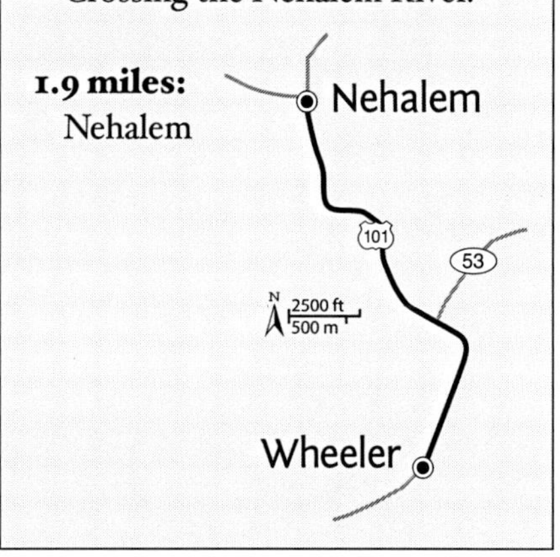

- **Wheeler Drugstore**
  (Rorvik and Nehalem)
  Operating since 1914. A dentist used to practice on the second floor.

- **The Old Wheeler Theatre**
  (Nehalem Avenue near the drugstore)
  Guido's Ristorante today.

Nehalem

Elevation: 41 feet

Location:
45.43.074 N • 123.53.693 W

Services:
gas, food, lodging, RV

Both the river and town are named in honor of the Nehalem Indian Tribe. The post office opened in 1870 under the name of August, changing to Onion Peak in 1884 and then to Nehalem in 1899. When driving downtown, you will see the businesses are built on stilts, several feet above the ground level as a precaution against floods. Several antique stores, clothing stores, and a bookstore cater to tourists.

downtown Nehalem

Points of Interest

- **Tillamook County Historical Site** *(7th and Tohls)*
  A marker, placed by the city of Nehalem on a Public Dock, designates the site of the first city dock). The City Hall and restrooms are nearby.

- **Nehalem Elementary School** *(8th and C)*
  The school was built in 1910. The words union high school are inscribed above the front doors.

- **Old Houses** *(between 8th and 9th on H Street)*
  Several of Nehalem's oldest residences.

- **Old Nehalem Elementary School** *(9th between A and B)*
  The old elementary school was built 1907 and now houses Tillamook Community College.

- **Nehalem United Methodist Church** *(10th and G)*
  Circa 1905.

- **Nehalem City Park** *(Hugo Street)*
  A large park with picnicking.

- **Nehalem State Park** *(three miles south of Manzanita Junction on Garey)*
  The only state park in Oregon with its own airstrip. Camping, hiking, horseback riding.

Nehalem to Elsie

Distance:
32.7 miles

Directions:
Travel northeast on North Fork Road. Caution: Travelers may wish to end the trip at Nehalem. If continuing, the next section of road contains 11.5 miles of well-maintained gravel and affords an alternate route over the coastal mountains, returning to Highway 26 near Elsie. It is not advisable to navigate this section of road during the winter.

Points En Route

(mileage from the corner of Highway 101 and Riverside Drive)

0.6 miles:
Nehalem Shores RV Park. Boat launch, store.

1.4 miles:
Turn right on McDonald Road. Cross the Nehalem River.

1.9 miles:
Homes constructed on stilts because of flooding.

2.7 miles:
Turn right on Highway 53 and travel toward Wheeler.

3.2 miles:
White Clover Grange Hall #784.

4.0 miles:
Mohler. (see page 49)

4.1 miles:
Turn left on Foss Creek Road. Look for an old two-story home.

5.4 miles:
Boat Launch, primitive toilets.

7.1 miles:
Former settlement of Foss. The post office operated from 1928 to 1943, and was named for Herbert Foss, who owned stands of timber here.

9.0 miles:
Road narrows with no shoulder.

9.2 miles:
Rock quarry.

10.5 miles:
Precarious crossing of the RR tracks.

11.8 miles:
Pavement ends. Gravel is well maintained with intermittent stretches of asphalt.

12.0 miles:
Waterfalls on the left.

12.1 miles:
Nehalem Falls Campground. Nehalem Falls are the highest falls in the Coast Range Mountains. Primitive toilets, hand pumped drinking water, firewood for sale, picnic sites and firepots. Group camping available. Foss Creek Road will soon become Lower Nehalem Road.

18.8 miles:
Site of Salmonberry, named for the orange-pink berries that thrive here.

19.0 miles:
River access.

22.0 miles:
Campground. Reduced speed.

22.6 miles:
A railroad car that has been transformed into a summer home.

23.3 miles:
More camping.

24.1 miles:
Campground.

26.3 miles:
Pavement returns.

26.5 miles:
Henry Ryerson Spruce Run Campground in the Clatsop State Forest.

30.0 miles:
Two lane, striped pavement returns.

31.0 miles:
Bridge over Humbug Creek.

32.4 miles:
Intersection with Highway 26. Turn left toward Seaside.

32.7 miles:
Elsie

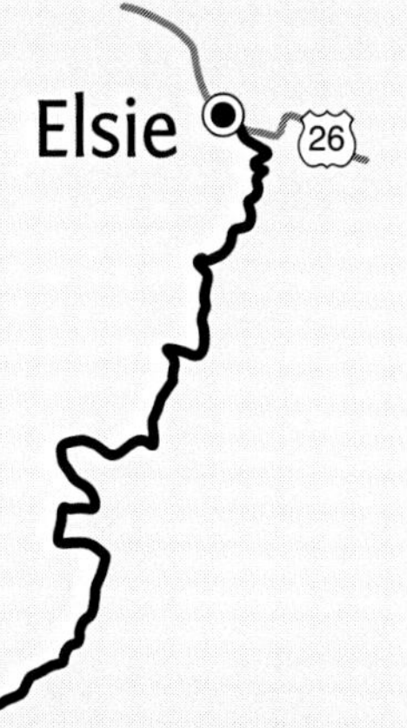

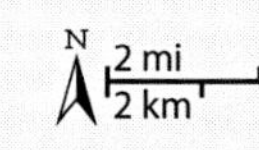

Elsie

Elevation: 505 feet

Location:
45.86.583 N • 123.59.361 W

Services:
food

The Elsie post office opened in 1892 and closed in 1943. Postmaster George Gragg wanted to name the community Clover, but that name was not accepted by postal authorities. Gragg submitted the name of Elsie, a close relative, and it was approved. The local economy is dependent on timber and tourism. Little remains of Elsie, which boasted several mills in its heyday.

Points of Interest

- **Camp 18** *(3 miles west on HW 26)*
  Restaurant and logging museum.
- **Sunny Hill Cemetery** *(take Elsie Cemetery Road, 4 miles east on Highway 26)*
  Dates to the 1880s

road to Elsie

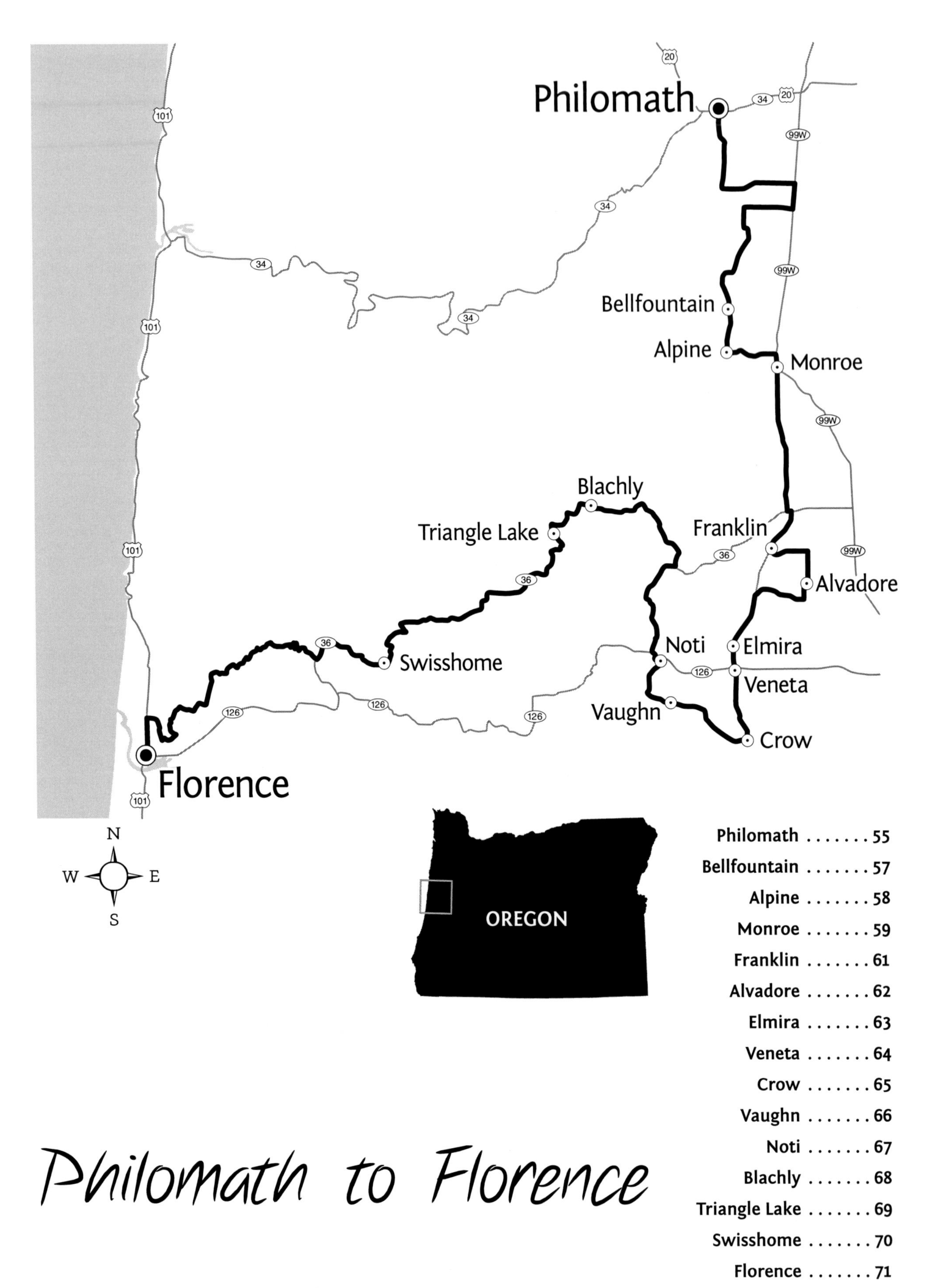

Philomath to Florence

In Search of Wisdom and Basketball Trophies

Philomath to Florence (127 miles)

From the western edge of the Willamette Valley to the central coast of Oregon, the roads less traveled, from Highway 34 to Highway 101, wind through fertile farmlands and recreation sites, and over the Coast Range Mountains to the beaches near Florence. Numerous mills, now silenced, rest quietly in various stages of decay. Old farms dot the landscape, forming quadrants of land, cut by roads that once connected crops to market.

The ebb and flow of the tides, the frequent winds and rain constantly reshape and reform the changing coastline. Elk, deer, eagles and ospreys frequently appear near the back road over the mountains. This trip begins in Philomath, which means 'love of learning,' ventures through Bellfountain and Alpine en route to Monroe, named for our fifth president. From Monroe travel south toward Elmira and drive west over the coast range to Florence, an important and growing city on the Central Oregon Coast.

rail road bridge between Vaughn and Noti

Philomath

Elevation: 279 feet

Location:
44.32.431 N • 123.22.265 W

Services:
gas, food, lodging

Philomath College

Philomath is a Greek word meaning 'love of learning.' Chartered in 1865 and opened in 1867, Philomath College was founded by the United Brethren Church. Constructed of locally made bricks, the oldest structure has two-foot thick walls. Philomath College was co-educational, providing a liberal arts education with an emphasis on ministerial training. Because of a rift in the church, a second college was constructed and named College of Philomath. Opening in 1889, this college burned twice and was last rebuilt in 1913. Lack of adequate funding during the depression forced both colleges to close in 1929. The center building of the older and larger Philomath College serves as a museum while the smaller College of Philomath building is undergoing restoration. The Philomath post office opened in 1867 and the town was named for the college. Most of the older homes in town were constructed on the north side of the highway.

Points of Interest

- **Railroad Caboose** *(Highway 20 near east entrance to town)*
  The Philomath Chamber of Commerce is housed in an old Southern Pacific caboose that rests on the grounds of an old mill. Open seasonally.

- **Mary's River Park** *(off Applegate between 9th and 11th)*
  A large park situated on Mary's River.

- **College of Philomath** *(10th and Pioneer)*
  The smaller of the two schools, it sits on a hill within view of the first school.

- **Philomath College** *(1101 Main Street)*
  Now the Benton County Museum. Free admission.

- **Old Philomath Hotel** *(226 N 13th)*
  An old, two-story structure near the railroad tracks. It is now a residence.

- **IOOF Hall** *(13th and College)*
  Constructed circa 1910.

- **Philomath Community Church** *(145 N 14th)*
  Built in the early 1900s. The old parsonage sits adjacent to the church at 131 N 14th.

- **Old House** *(1547 Applegate)*
  This home was constructed in 1910.

Old Philomath Hotel

College of Philomath

- **Old Philomath School**
  (19th and Ash)
  Built in 1902.

- **Philomath City Park**
  (23rd Street)
  Playground, picnic area, and restrooms.

- **Mt. Union Cemetery**
  (Mt. Union Avenue)
  Dates to the 1870s.

- **Gathering Together Farms**
  (24659 Grange Hall Road)
  Organic farm and year-round store.

- **Green Gables Gardens**
  (24689 Grange Hall Road)
  This beautiful home was built in the 1930s.

- **Mary's River Grange #685**
  (27407 Grange Hall Road)
  1920s construction.

- **Mary's Peak**
  8.6 miles west of town, the 4097 feet peak is located up an 11.6 mile, winding road.

Philomath to Bellfountain

Distance:
21.7 miles

Directions:
From 13th and Main, go south.

Points En Route

(mileage from 13th and Main)

0.3 miles:
Philomath Rodeo Grounds.

0.7 miles:
Crossing Evergreen Creek.

0.7 miles:
Grange Hall Road.

3.2 miles:
An old school house identified as Independent School District #19.

4.9 miles:
Intersection with Llewellyn Road. The site of Fern, which had a post office from 1899 to 1903.

5.0 miles:
Possibly the old Fern Schoolhouse.

6.3 miles:
Intersection with Bellfountain Road. Continue on Llewellyn toward Highway 99.

9.6 miles:
Intersection with Highway 99. Turn right and drive south on Highway 99.

11.1 miles:
Greenberry Road. Turn right and drive west. The historic Willamette Community Hall and Grange are at this intersection.

13.5 miles:
Tyee Wine Cellars, producing wines since 1985.

14.2 miles:
Intersection with Bellfountain Road. Go left and drive south to Bellfountain.

17.8 miles:
William Finley Wildlife Refuge. Namesake William Finley was a state biologist and game warden, and the first member of the Oregon Fish and Game Commission. This is the largest game refuge in Oregon, covering more than 5,000 acres. Three major hiking trails range from 1.2 to 4 miles in length. Numerous rare and endangered species live in the refuge; most notable are the Fenders blue butterfly and Kincaids lupine. Eagles and elk are frequently spotted in the refuge.

20.9 miles:
Intersection with Bell Road. Continue on Bellfountain Road.

21.7 miles:
Bellfountain

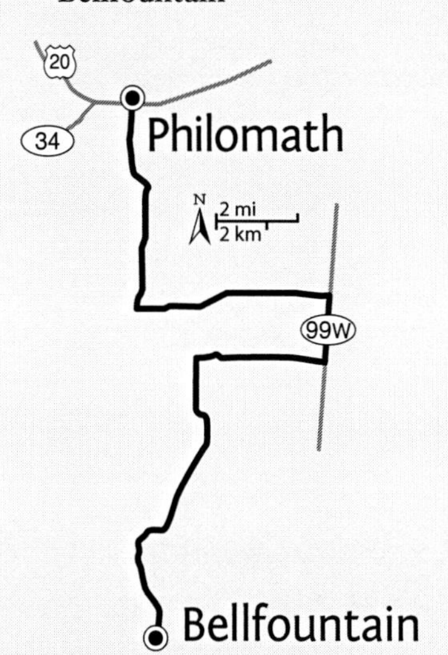

Bellfountain

Elevation: 322 feet

Location:
44.21.823 N • 123.21.331 W

Services:
none

The first post office was established in 1895 as Dusty, then was changed to Bellfountain (from Bellfountaine, Ohio) in 1902. This post office closed in 1905. Tiny Bellfountain High School – it was never more than fifty students during its existence – made an incredible athletic stir in 1937, when its basketball team beat Portland's Lincoln High School 35-12, to win the state championship. The team was coached by Bill Lemon, and is Oregon's version of the Hoosiers.

Bellfountain School

Points of Interest

- **Bellfountain School**
  Now the Cornerstone Christian School, the building was constructed in 1906. The 1937 State Basketball trophy is displayed inside the front doors, sitting high in a trophy case near the entrance to the school.

- **Applegate Trail Marker**
  Next to the old Bellfountain School gym, marking the Southern Route of the Jesse Applegate's Oregon Trail.

- **Bellfountain Community Church**
  Built in 1901, the church was founded by four circuit riders, who alternated preaching duties on subsequent Sundays. The church was constructed with beautiful stained glass windows.

- **Bellfountain Cemetery**
  (0.8 miles east on Bellfountain Road)
  Dates to the early 1900s.

- **Bellfountain County Park**
  (1.0 miles west on Dawson Road)
  This was the site of summer Methodist Church Revival meetings in the early 1900s.

- **Hull-Oakes Mill**
  (3.0 miles west on Dawson Road)
  The pavement ends at the only steam driven lumber mill in Oregon.

Bellfountain to Alpine

Distance:
2.4 miles

Directions:
From the old store at intersection of Bellfountain Road and Dawson Road, go south on Bellfountain Road.

Points En Route

(mileage from intersection of Bellfountain Road and Dawson Road)

This route follows the Benton County Scenic Loop.

0.4 miles:
Two old farmhouses.

2.4 miles:
Alpine

Bellfountain

N 2500 ft 500 m

Alpine

Bellfountain Community Church

Alpine

Elevation: 219 feet

Location:
44.19.748 N • 123.21.615 W

Services:
food (if store is open), tavern

Named for the alpine forest that once covered the area, this Benton County community shares its name with a community in Morrow County. The post office was established in 1912.

Alpine Market

Alpine parking meter

Points of Interest

- **Alpine Market**
  Opened in 1908. Now closed, there is a parking meter in front of the store.

- **Alpine Tavern and Pool Hall**
  The tavern opened in the 1920s, catering to the hearty and thirsty timber workers.

- **Alpine Cemetery**
  (0.2 miles west of town)
  Parts of the cemetery are covered with Astroturf.

- **Glenbrook**
  (8.0 miles west on Alpine Road)
  This small community had its own post office in 1898.

Alpine to Monroe

Distance:
3.4 miles

Directions:
From the intersection of Bellfountain Road and Alpine Road, drive east toward Monroe.

Points En Route

(mileage from the Alpine Market)

2.3 miles:
Turn right on Alpine Cut-off Road.

3.2 miles:
Intersection with Highway 99. Turn right.

3.4 miles:
Monroe

Alpine
99W
2500 ft
500 m
Monroe

Monroe

Elevation: 288 feet

Location:
44.18.873 N • 123.17.900 W

Services:
gas, food

Named for President James Monroe, the community was platted on an 1846 land claim owned by Joseph White, who built a sawmill near the river in 1850. The post office opened in 1852 under the name of Starr's Point. Starr's Point was named for George Starr, who owned and ran the store. The name was changed to Monroe in 1874 and the community incorporated in 1914.

House in Monroe

Points of Interest

- **Monroe High School**
  The school was constructed in 1906. The Applegate Trail crossed directly in front of the where the school building stands.

- **Toddler Park** *(6th and Main adjacent to an old school building)*
  A unique playground designed for small children.

- **Three-Story House**
  (6th and Commercial)
  Ornate streetlights surround this home that has a large cupola.

- **United Methodist Church**
  (650 Orchard)
  The church is over 150 years old. The old parsonage lies in ruin behind the church building.

- **Monroe Cemetery**
  (Cemetery Hill)
  With a commanding a view above the town, this old cemetery dates to the 1860s.

- **St. Rose Cemetery** *(Coon Road)*
  An 1885 Catholic Memorial Park.

- **St. Rose of Lima Catholic Church** *(Territorial and Dragon)*
  Built in 1883.

- **Monroe Brick Yard**
  (Reiling Road)
  The brick-baking ovens are a reminder of the old factory. Sternwheelers would dock at the river and load brick for distribution to Eugene, Salem and Portland.

- **Railroad Tracks**
  (beneath 6th Street)
  Rather than remove the tracks, the city paved over them, leaving rails showing through the street.

- **Monroe Bank** *(corner of Highway 99 and Commercial)*
  The bank was built in 1911 with an old clock displayed above the front entrance.

United Methodist Church

Monroe Brick Yard

- **Monroe Museum** *(120 Main)* Preserves the history of south Benton County.
- **Old Monroe Market** *(160 Main)* Freezer lockers line the back of this building, which is now a barbershop.
- **Old Dam** *(Commercial and Highway 99)* Concrete foundations where a dam that once generated power for a gristmill.

Cheshire water tower

Monroe to Franklin

Distance:
11.6 miles

Directions:
From the intersection of Highway 99 and Commercial, go south on Highway 99.

Points En Route

(mileage from the corner of Commercial and Highway 99)

This road follows the Applegate Rail and the old Territorial Road to California.

0.1 miles:
Turn right onto Territorial Road, traveling south.

1.8 miles:
Benton Lane Winery, known for its Pinot Noir.

2.1 miles:
Entering Lane County.

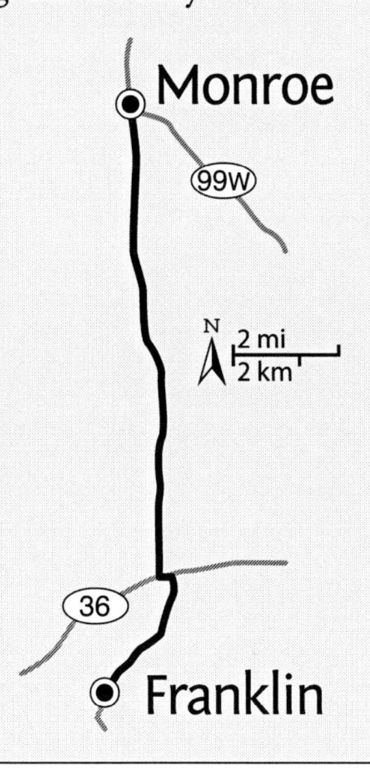

3.2 miles:
Diamond Woods Golf Course.

4.6 miles:
Site of Ferguson, named after the pioneer family that settled here.

6.5 miles:
Rest Lawn Cemetery, dates to the mid 1880s.

7.0 miles:
Danish Cemetery (to the right).

8.8 miles:
Cheshire. Initially a station on the Southern Pacific Railroad Line, the town was platted as Hubert in 1913. The railroad changed the name to Cheshire as a compliment to Hubert Cheshire, a young boy in the community. The Hubert post office opened in March of 1914 with the name changing to Cheshire two months later.

8.8 miles:
At the junction of Territorial and Highway 36, turn right, traveling east.

9.0 miles:
Turn right onto the Cheshire Cut-off road and drive south toward Franklin. This road was part of the Southern Route of the Oregon Trail, often referred to as the Applegate Trail.

11.6 miles:
Franklin

Franklin

Elevation: 435 feet

Location:
44.09.565 N • 123.18.400 W

Services:
none

The Franklin-Smithfield post office was established in 1855. The name Smithfield was officially dropped in the 1960s, ending more than one hundred years of fighting to keep it included. The Smithfield name came from 1852-53 pioneer Daniel Smith. Another community in Polk County had registered the name of Smithfield, thus postal officials changed the name to Franklin. Some longtime residents remember the fight and still use the original name.

Bethany Church of Franklin

Points of Interest

- **Franklin Grange**
  (92081 Territorial Highway)
  Center of community activity.

- **Bethany Church of Franklin**
  Serving the Franklin community.
  Constructed in 1897.

- **Franklin Christian Church**
  (adjacent to the Bethany Church)
  This church was built in 1900.

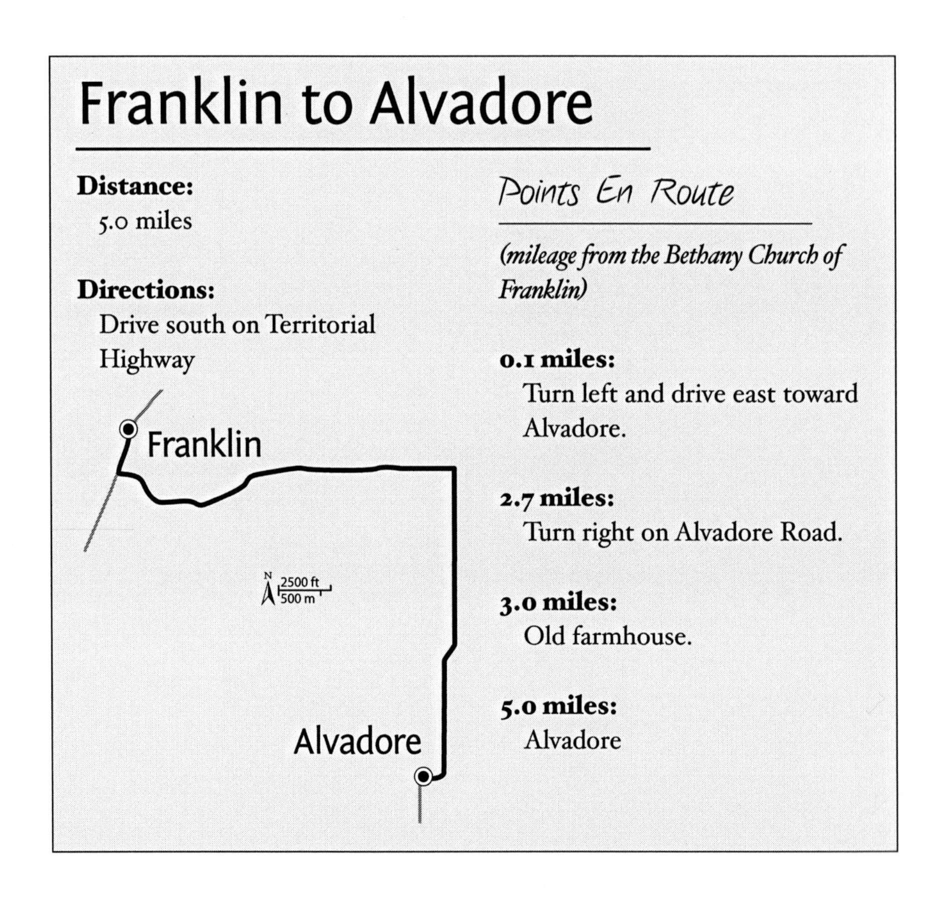

Franklin to Alvadore

Distance:
5.0 miles

Directions:
Drive south on Territorial Highway

Points En Route

(mileage from the Bethany Church of Franklin)

0.1 miles:
Turn left and drive east toward Alvadore.

2.7 miles:
Turn right on Alvadore Road.

3.0 miles:
Old farmhouse.

5.0 miles:
Alvadore

Alvadore

Elevation: 390 feet

Location:
44.07.586 N • 123.15.893 W

Services:
gas, food

Ten miles north and west of Eugene, Alvadore was named to honor Alvadore Welch, a public utility manager who brought the Portland, Eugene and Eastern Railway to this locale. The Alvadore post office opened in 1914 and was a bustling community that had a fine hotel and several businesses. Rail service ended in the early 1930s, the tracks were removed in 1936, and the town suffered as the result. The beautiful, turn of the century school building was dismantled in 2006.

Alvadore Store

Points of Interest

- **Main Street**
  The former center of commerce, where the hotel and businesses once stood, is now a cherry orchard.

- **Railroad Avenue**
  Rails long ago removed, the tracks ran in front of the Blue Diamond Hazelnut dryers.

Alvadore to Elmira

Distance:
7.5 miles

Directions:
From the general store, travel south on Alvadore Road.

Points En Route

(mileage from the Alvadore Store)

0.8 miles:
Turn right on Clear Lake Road and drive west.

1.3 miles:
Orchard Point Park, on Fern Ridge Reservoir. Native Bracken and Sword ferns are abundant.

1.5 miles:
Lane County Marina and boat launch.

2.7 miles:
Fern Ridge Dam and spillway.

3.9 miles:
Richardson Park and Applegate Interpretive Center.

4.1 miles:
Turn left on Territorial Highway and drive south.

7.5 miles:
Elmira

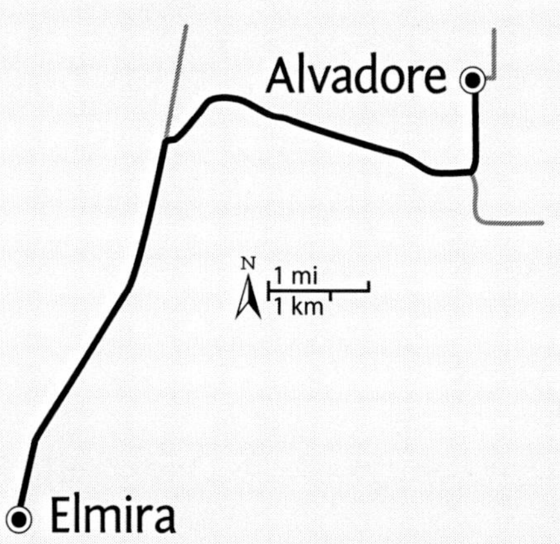

Elmira

Elevation: 399 feet

Location:
44.04.039 N • 123.21.243 W

Services:
food, gas

Elmira IOOF Hall

Byron Ellmaker, who greatly missed and admired his hometown, named the community after Elmira, California. Ellmaker bought a section of land in 1880 on which he built a wood and iron forge. It was near the present location of downtown Elmira, which was then called Duckworth. Ellmaker convinced authorities to change the name from Duckworth to Elmira in 1884. Elmira is close to the Long Tom River and Fern Ridge Reservoir. Elmira has never officially incorporated. Wineries and vineyards are providing an economic boost to the area.

Points of Interest

- **Elmira School District Office**
  (Territorial and Warthen)
  Located in the 1914 schoolhouse.

- **Elmira Store and Gas**
  (24957 Warthen Road)
  The old store is now the Elmira Locker Service.

- **Elmira Grange #593**
  (88964 Sprague)
  The aging grange hall is still in use.

- **Elmira IOOF Hall #207**
  (24961 Horn)
  The vacant lodge is in need of restoration.

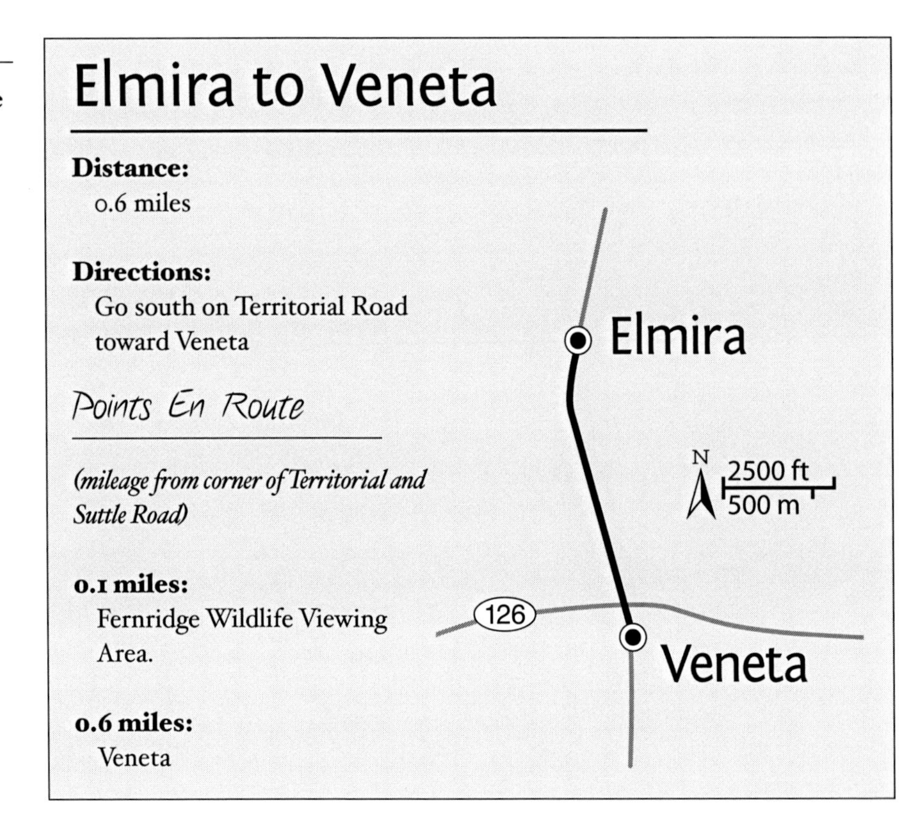

Elmira to Veneta

Distance:
0.6 miles

Directions:
Go south on Territorial Road toward Veneta

Points En Route

(mileage from corner of Territorial and Suttle Road)

0.1 miles:
Fernridge Wildlife Viewing Area.

0.6 miles:
Veneta

Veneta

Elevation: 420 feet

Location:
44.03.073 N • 123.21.543 W

Services:
food, gas

E.E. Hunter, who named Veneta after his five-year-old daughter, formed and platted the town in 1912. The post office was established in 1913. Veneta incorporated in 1962 and has a population of about 5,000. Veneta Hunter passed away in 2000. Several wineries are located nearby and the Lane County Fair is held near this small community.

Applegate Pioneer Museum

Points of Interest

- **Ralph Johnson Park**
  (5th and Dunham)
  Named for Veneta's first mayor.

- **Applegate Pioneer Museum**
  (Broadway and 7th)
  The building was once the Crow School, moved to this site. Some Crow residents are still angry the school was moved out of town.

- **City Park** *(east end of Broadway)*
  5.9 acres that includes the Veneta Pool, which opened in 2010.

- **Western Forestry Center**
  (8700 block of Territorial)
  Maps, tree and firewood permits, and general information about forest practices.

- **Our Daily Bread**
  (88170 Territorial)
  An old church converted into a bakery and café.

- **Veneta Skate Park**
  (between McCutcheon and Meadowvale on Territorial)
  A layout that challenges the skills of every skater.

- **Territorial Park**
  (Territorial and Hunter)
  2.5-acre neighborhood park with skate park, basketball court, picnic area and restrooms.

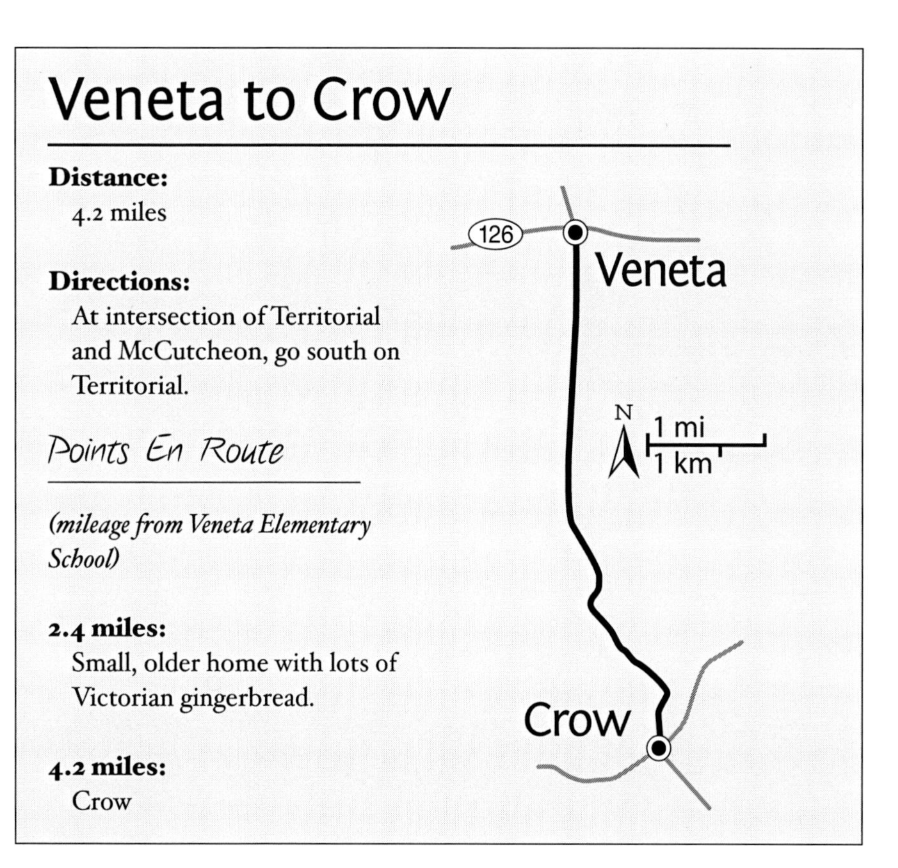

Veneta to Crow

Distance:
4.2 miles

Directions:
At intersection of Territorial and McCutcheon, go south on Territorial.

Points En Route

(mileage from Veneta Elementary School)

2.4 miles:
Small, older home with lots of Victorian gingerbread.

4.2 miles:
Crow

Crow

Elevation: 620 feet

Location:
43.59.517 N • 123.20.215 W

Services:
food, gas

The town was named after James Andrew Jackson Crow, pioneer settler who came to Oregon by wagon train and co-founded the community. The post office was established in November 6, 1874. Crow is also the literal translation of an Indian word, *andaig*, which has to do with the locality. Crow is an unincorporated community. Wild turkeys are frequently seen in the area.

Crow-Hadleyville Church of the Nazarene

Points of Interest

- **Crow Market and Gas**
  Displayed inside are photos of the town's old school and church. The old two-story schoolhouse and the old church once stood behind the store.

- **Crow Grange #455**
  The hall was built in 1911.

- **Crow School**
  The school was constructed in 1916.

- **Crow Cemetery**
  0.2 miles from the store.

- **Crow-Hadleyville Church of the Nazarene** *(0.8 miles on Territorial to the intersection with Crow Road)*
  This majestic church building was erected on the side of a hill.

- **Hadleyville** *(1.7 miles south and east of town off of the Territorial Highway on Battle Creek Road)*
  Hadleyville had it's own post office in 1890. The 1922 Coyote Creek Covered Bridge leads to the former settlement. In the 1840s, members of the Applegate Trail party killed coyotes here.

- **Briggs Hill School** *(4.5 miles south on Territorial)*
  Now a private residence. On the hills north and south of the school, wagon ruts of the Applegate Trail are still visible.

- **Hinman and Sweet Cheeks Wineries** *(from the old Briggs School, continue 0.3 miles north on Briggs Hill Road.)*
  Both have tasting rooms.

Coyote Creek Covered Bridge

Vaughn

Elevation: 499 feet

Location:
44.01.293 N • 123.25.583 W

Services:
none

Sidner Vaughn, the town's namesake, homesteaded near the mouth of this creek in 1891. Vaughn Creek empties into Dorena Reservoir which flooded the town of Dorena in 1949.

Points of Interest

- **Rosboro Lumber Company**
  (both sides of Crow-Vaughn Road)
  A large mill that remains open. Many such mills once dotted the area.

old bus depot

Crow to Vaughn

Distance:
5.6 miles

Directions:
At the intersection of Territorial and Vaughn Road, go west on Vaughn.

Points En Route

3.6 miles:
Old home and barn.

5.6 miles:
Vaughn

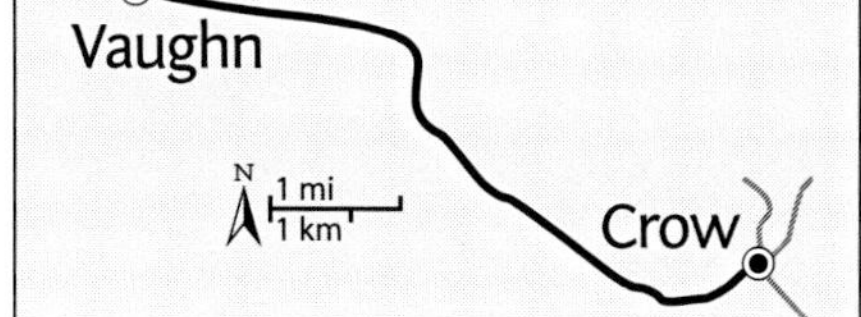

Rosboro Lumber Company

Vaughn to Noti

Distance:
3.9 miles

Directions:
From the Rosboro Forest Products Mill, travel northwest toward Noti.

Points En Route

(mileage from the Rosboro Mill pipes that cross over the road)

0.8 miles:
Stop. Railroad tracks.

2.2 miles:
Two small but noteworthy homes.

3.9 miles:
Noti

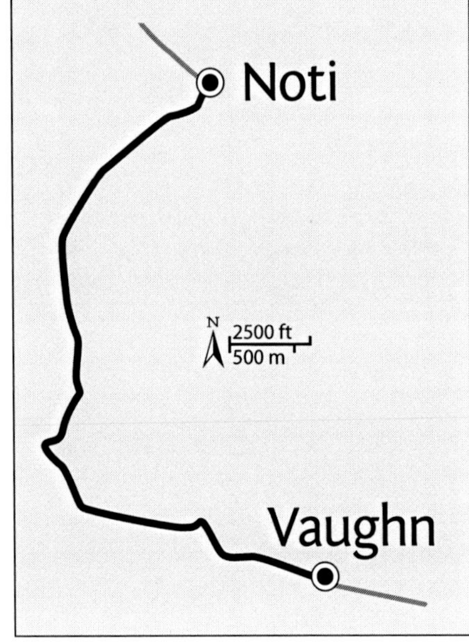

Noti

Elevation: 440 feet

Location:
44.03.481 N • 123.26.880 W

Services:
gas, food

Noti School

As the story goes, two people were riding one horse; the agreement was for one to ride two miles, then tie up the horse and allow the person walking to catch up, then untie the horse and repeat the process with the other rider. Noti gets its name as a result of one of the riders failing to tie up the horse, or 'No Tie.' Noti is an unincorporated community in Lane County. The name of the community changed from Portola to Noti when the post office opened in 1913. Highway 126 was constructed in 1996, by-passing the community.

Points of Interest

- **Swanson Brothers Lumber Mill** *(intersection of Highway 126 and Crow-Vaughn Road)*
  Doing business since 1937.

- **Noti General Store** *(corner of Crow-Vaughn Road and Noti-Loop Road)*
  The store opened in the 1930s. The post office, which stands next door, originally housed in the store.

- **Noti School** *(bottom of hill on the Crow-Vaughn Road)*
  The large, two-story school was built in 1921. The public school closed in 2002 and is now a head start center. The school was moved to this location when the new highway was constructed in 1996.

Swanson Brothers Lumber Mill

Noti to Blachly

Distance:
16.2 miles

Directions:
Travel northwest on Noti-Loop Road.

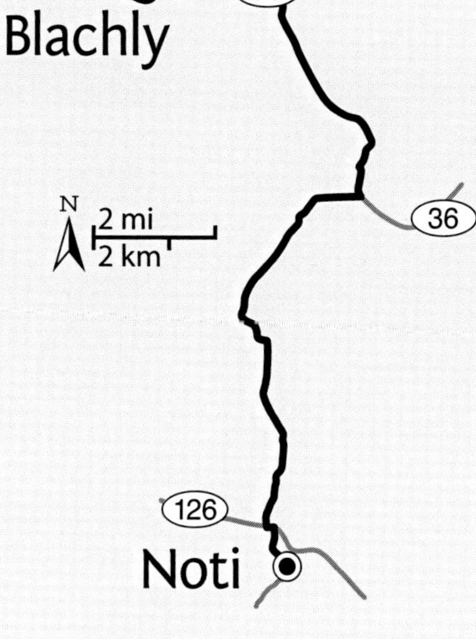

Points En Route

(mileage from the Noti Market)

0.8 miles:
Turn left and travel west on Highway 126.

0.9 miles:
Turn right on Poodle Creek Road and travel north toward Triangle Lake.

6.2 miles:
Logging clear cuts.

7.3 miles:
Camp Serene, a Lutheran Retreat Center.

7.7 miles:
Turn left; drive west on Highway 36.

8.6 miles:
Alderwood State Wayside. Day use only; picnic and restrooms.

8.8 miles:
(intersection of Hall Road and Highway 36) Site of Burp Hollow.

9.7 miles:
Camp Sherwood.

11.6 miles:
Low Pass, gas and grocery, on the Long Tom River.

16.2 miles:
Blachly

Blachly

Elevation: 717 feet

Location:
44.11.694 N • 123.32.036 W

Services:
none

The Blachly post office opened in 1892 and was named for resident William Blachly. Blachly was born in Illinois in 1844, came to Oregon in 1854 and passed away at his residence in 1934, three days after his 90th birthday. Triangle Lake Schools serve the small unincorporated community.

Points of Interest

- **Laughing Rabbit Industries**
  (20448 Highway 36)
  Famous for making Photon Lights, LRI is housed in the old Blachly General Store, built in the early 1900s.

- **The Green House**
  (across from post office)
  Constructed in 1907.

- **The White House**
  Affectionately named by locals, was built in 1922.

old Blachly General Store

Blachly to Triangle Lake

Distance:
3.0 miles

Directions:
From the old Blachly General Store, continue west on Highway 36.

Points En Route

(mileage from the old store and Highway 36)

0.4 miles:
Triangle Lake Schools. The earliest construction dates to 1921. Nearby is the Triangle Lake Grange #533. The hall opened in 1922 and served as the community church on Sundays.

0.9 miles:
Old home at the corner of Post Road and Highway 36. The Blachly Cemetery is located up Post Road.

1.9 miles:
A round barn and pheasant farm.

3.0 miles:
Triangle Lake

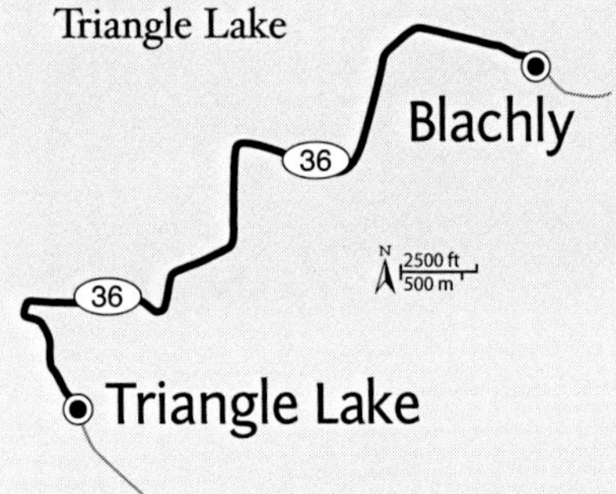

Triangle Lake

Elevation: 702 feet

Location:
44.10.417 N • 123.34.867 W

Services:
food

Triangle Lake, which covers 293 acres, was named for its shape. It had been called Loon Lake, Lake of the Woods and Echo Lake before changing for the last time in 1900. Kokanee salmon, cutthroat trout, largemouth bass, bluegill, yellow perch, brown bullhead, and pumpkinseed thrive in its waters. Run-off from the lake empties into Lake Creek, keeping the lake at a fixed and constant level. Younger than Blachly, Triangle Lake has more vacation homes than year-round residents. The Triangle Lake store, the only business in the community, burned in May of 2007 and was rebuilt in 2009. Triangle Lake has not incorporated.

Points of Interest

Note: All homes and businesses in Triangle Lake stand along the highway. The places are in order as the traveler would see them along this route.

- **Triangle Lake Park County Park**
  Restrooms, boat launch, picnic, fishing.
- **Triangle Lake Community Church**
  Built in 1953.
- **Oregon Department of Forestry**
  Relatively new construction.
- **Triangle Lake Conference Center**
  Built in the 1970s.

Triangle Lake

Triangle Lake to Swisshome

Distance:
17.7 miles

Directions:
From the Triangle Lake Community Church, drive south on Highway 36.

Points En Route

(mileage from the church)

0.3 miles:
Triangle Lake Park. Camping, picnicking, restrooms, fishing.

0.5 miles:
State Rest Area. A trail leads to a natural water slide.

2.8 miles:
Garden of Peace Monastery.

3.1 miles:
Elk Mountain Ranch.

4.5 miles:
Greeleaf Creek.

5.7 miles:
Century Farm.

7.5 miles:
Greenleaf. Not named for a person, but for the beauty of the area. The description was first used in 1885 to describe the community. The post office was established about 1892. A nearby creek shares the same name and flows into Lake Creek.

8.3 miles:
Nelson Creek Road and Nelson Creek Covered Bridge.

12.6 miles:
Deadwood: gas, food. The community's name, which describes an area covered with snags as a result of a forest fire, come in 1884 when the post office opened. The local cemetery is en route to a 1932 covered bridge, 5.0 miles north on Deadwood Creek Road.

15.2 miles:
Site of Indiola, a former logging community.

15.4 miles:
Schindler, a Lane County Park. Boat ramp, picnic area and fishing. Primitive restrooms.

17.7 miles:
Swisshome

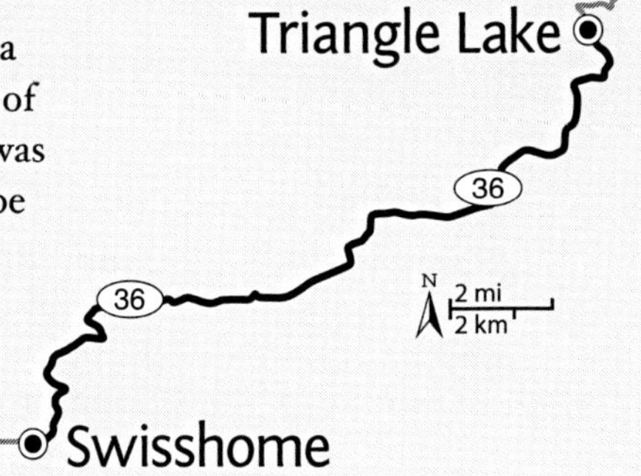

Swisshome

Elevation: 150 feet

Location:
44.10.416 N • 123.34.866 W

Services:
gas, food

Swiss settlers named Swisshome, a small agricultural community. The post office was established in 1902. The first postmaster was Heinrich Zwiedler who hailed from Switzerland. Swisshome was a logging and wood products community until the decline of the timber industry.

Points of Interest

- **Swisshome Evangelical Church**
  Old, but still in use.

Nelson Creek Covered Bridge

Swisshome to Florence

Distance:
24.1 miles

Directions:
From the store, drive west on Highway 36.

Points En Route

(mileage from the store)

1.0 miles:
Old sawmill burner.

2.3 miles:
Tide Wayside, a Lane County Park.

4.5 miles:
Site of Brickerville.

4.8 miles:
Turn right onto North Fork Siuslaw Road, which follows the Old Stagecoach Road and has 3.6 miles of gravel. For those not wishing to drive on gravel, stay on Highway 36 to Florence.

5.3 miles:
Pavement ends. Well-maintained gravel for 3.6 miles.

7.1 miles:
Keep right.

8.9 miles:
Pioneer Trail Marker. Pavement returns.

9.9 miles:
Site of Minerva, named after the wife of pioneer James Bay.

11.1 miles:
Siuslaw Valley Fire and Rescue Station.

11.3 miles:
Intersection of North Fork Siuslaw Road and North Fork Road. Farm to the left is the Minerva Ranch. Turn left toward Florence.

19.6 miles:
Old homestead and Bender Landing, a Lane County Park with boat launch, picnic area, and restrooms.

21.9 miles:
Turn right on Munsel Lake Road.

22.1 miles:
Oregon Dunes Golf Course.

23.1 miles:
Munsel Park. Boat launch, picnic area, and restrooms.

24.0 miles:
Heceta Junction. Turn left toward Florence city center.

24.1 miles:
Florence

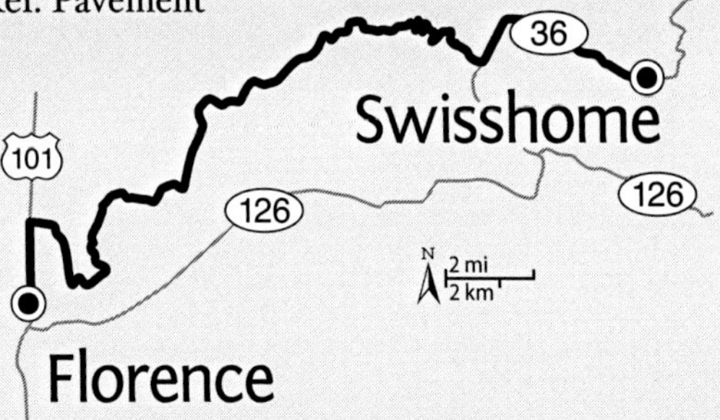

Florence

Elevation: 10 feet

Location:
43.59.301 N • 124.06.110 W

Services:
gas, food, lodging, B&B

The Siuslaw Tribe of Native Americans inhabited this area for as long as 12,000 years before making contact with white trappers in the 1820s. Even though the first permanent settlers came here in 1878 and the town was incorporated in 1893, few people lived in Florence until the first salmon cannery opened in 1900, followed two years later by the first sawmill. The community was named for A.B. Florence who represented Lane County from 1858-1862. In 1970 Florence received notoriety when state workers attempted to blow up a stranded whale found on the beach. The thinking of the day was that the dynamite would blow the whale in minute pieces providing important nourishment for nature's inhabitants. The debacle turned south when the explosion sent large chunks of rotting blubber everywhere. Today the community is a gateway to Oregon's southern coast and the expansive Oregon Sand Dune Recreational Area.

bridge and pilings in Florence

Points of Interest

- **Old Town Florence**
(between 1st and Bay)
The blocks adjacent to the waterfront form the town's historic district.

- **Callison Building** *(278 Maple)*
Constructed in 1905, this old-timer has seen many uses, including that of a schoolhouse. A 1953 fire destroyed the second story.

- **David House** *(232 Maple)*
One of Florence's earliest homes, built in 1906 by a local millwright, this is now a Bed and Breakfast. The house boasts of a sunburst influenced by Eastlake architecture.

- **Kyle and Sons Mercantile**
(Laurel and Bay)
This 1901 Italianate, false-front building, was the area's only mercantile store until it closed in 1961. It has since been remodeled to house a variety of shops as well as a restaurant.

Kyle and Sons Mercantile

- **Bridgewater Restaurant**
(Laurel and Bay)
The 1922 Mapleton Train Depot building was moved to this location in 1977.

- **Boon House** *(168 Maple)*
Erected in 1912, this was once a boarding house for bachelor loggers and fishermen.

- **Masonic Lodge and Building**
(corner of 1st and Maple)
Built in 1903.

- **Newspaper Office** *(148 Maple)*
The Siuslaw News. An old linotype greets patrons as they enter the building.

- **Spruce Point Museum**
(1.0 miles south of town, located at 85294 Highway 101)
Open seasonally, this museum offers a plethora of information on the area's history,

- **Sand Dune Recreational Area**
(3.0 miles south of Florence on west side of Highway 101)
Jesse Honeyman State Park provides access to some of the great dunes as well as camping, picnicking, fishing, and swimming.

- **Darlingtonia State Natural Wayside** *(3.0 miles north of town on Highway 101)*
Venus flytraps grow naturally in this botanical paradise that comes with a self-guided tour along wooden bridges.

- **Heceta Beach County Park**
(near the Darlingtonia Wayside)
Located on the west side of the highway, the park was named in honor of Bruno Heceta who, in 1775, was one of the West coast's earliest explorers.

Florence docks

- **Sea Lion Caves** *(7.3 miles north of town on Highway 101)*
An elevator leads down into a cave where sea lions live in their natural habitat.

- **Heceta Head Lighthouse**
(9.0 miles north of town on Highway 101)
Operational since 1894, this lighthouse sits on a point that juts into the Pacific Ocean. Bruno Heceta wrote in his journal about the shallow waters off the shoreline, and the point on which the lighthouse, which is named after him, is erected.

- **Freshwater Lakes**
More than a dozen freshwater lakes lie within fifteen miles of Florence. The largest, Siltcoos Lake, is known for perch and pan fish.

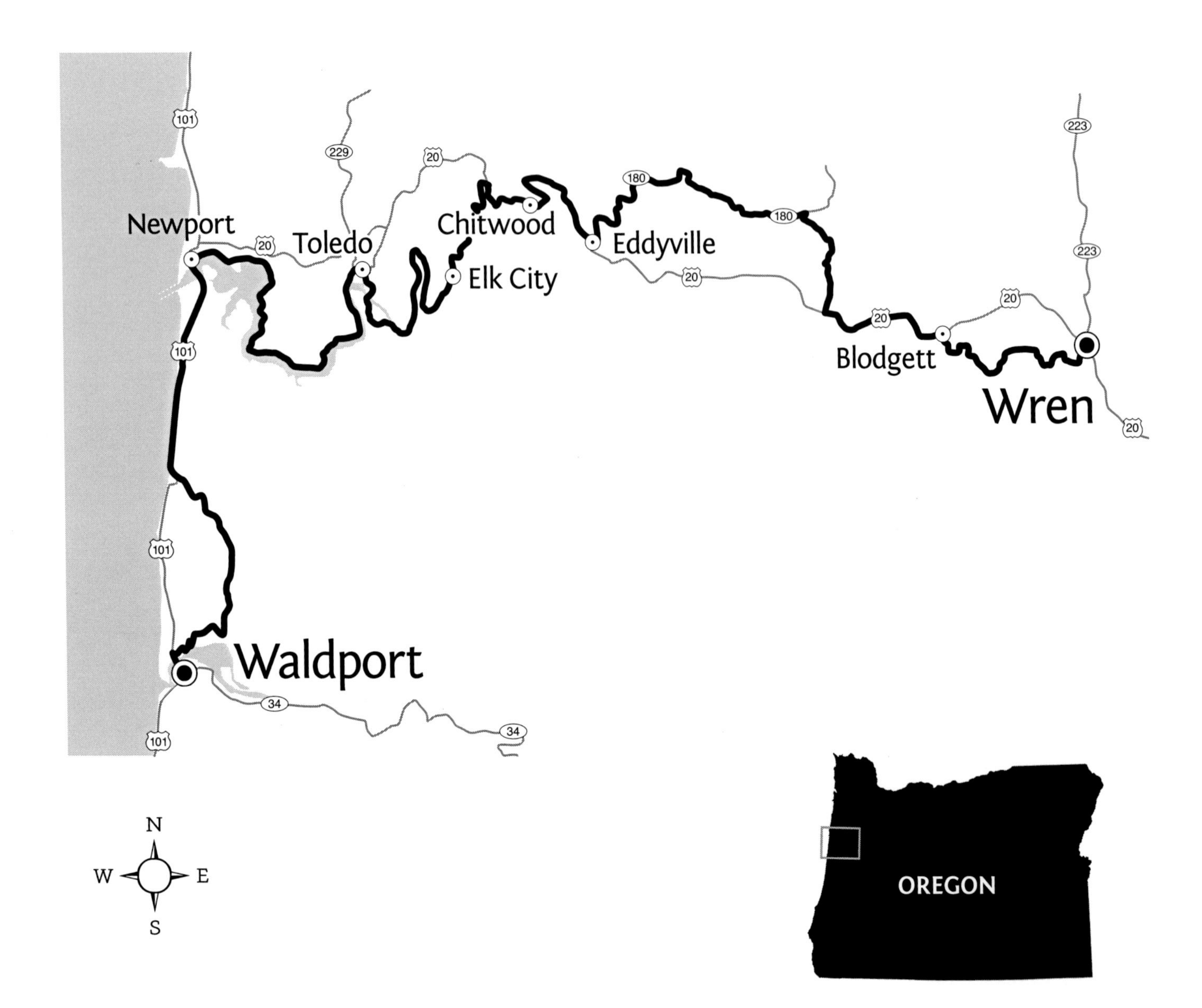

Waldport to Wren

Discovering Lesser Known Coastal Byways

Waldport to Wren (80 miles)

Before Highway 101 was constructed, car travel between communities on the coast was often accomplished by driving on the sandy beaches, which resulted in countless numbers of automobiles stuck in sand and damaged by corrosive salt water. Today, Highway 101, while frequently traveled, provides the main arterial for exploration onto the rural connecting roads that see few cars.

Once off the main highways, narrow two-lane ribbons of curving asphalt bring together the coast and the valley, with a five-mile section of gravel that followed an old stagecoach route, developed over one hundred years ago. This adventure begins in Waldport, a seaport community whose existence was rooted in lumber, and concludes in Wren, a foothills community east of the coast range that lived, prospered, and died by timber.

oyster shells along the road from Newport to Toledo

Waldport

Elevation: 31 feet

Location:
44.25.350 N • 124.04.317 W

Services:
gas, food, lodging, RV, B&B, camping

Waldport is a combination the German word *wald*, meaning forest, and the English word *port*. David Ruble settled the community in 1879, and its post office opened in 1881. The town was chartered in 1890 and had its own railroad line from 1918 until 1935. Fishing and lumber have been the economic mainstays of this small but growing community. Alsea Bay is among the five busiest in the state.

Alsea Bridge

Points of Interest

- **Alsea Bridge Interpretive Center** *(620 NW Spring, at the foot of the bridge)*
  The interpretive center gives the history of the bridge, has restrooms and a gift shop.

- **Old Waldport School**
  (between John and Cedar on Spring)
  The school opened in 1916.

- **Old Baptist Church** *(780 Bay)*
  Built in 1909 and now a private residence.

- **Early Waldport House**
  (225 Spencer)
  This 1909 two-story home has a unique widow's walk.

- **Port of Alsea**
  (Port and Broadway)
  Boat basin and boat launch area.

- **Old Town**
  (between Port and Spencer and Mill)
  The town grew around the mill. Old Town has a number of original storefronts.

- **Old Town Tavern**
  In operation since 1897.

- **Waldport Heritage Museum**
  (320 Grant)
  Lots of early Waldport photos are kept in this 1941 Civilian Conservation Corps Building. On the porch is a wooden water pipe from the city's early water line system.

Old Waldport School

- **Site of Harrison's Mill**
  (trailer park on Mill)
  Location of a huge mill that operated from the early 1900s through the 1970s.

- **Oldest Building in Waldport**
  (Ruble and Broadway)
  Built in 1895.

- **Old Residence** *(1040 Broadway)*
  A home constructed in 1910.

- **Old House** *(1060 Broadway)*
  Constructed in 1913.

- **Old Jail** *(Mill Street next to Hot Tubs and Heating)*
  The jail opened in 1910 and was moved to this site.

- **Site of the Opera House**
  (Mill and Ruble)
  The old opera house burned in 1967.

- **Alsea Hospital** *(above the high school on Hospital Hill)*
  Opened in the 1920s, now a private residence.

pillar on Alsea Bridge

Waldport to Newport

Distance:
16.3 miles

Directions:
At the intersection of Highway 101 and Highway 34, drive north on Highway 101.

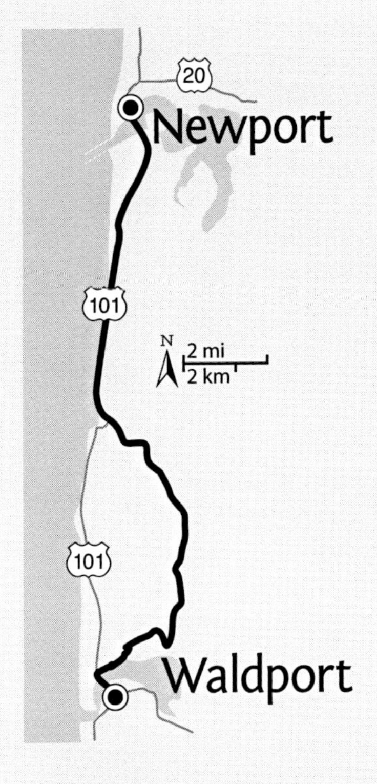

Points En Route

(mileage from the stop light at the intersection of Highway 101 and Highway 34)

0.8 miles:
After crossing the bridge, turn right on N. Bayview Road.

1.5 miles:
Expansive view high above the Alsea Estuary.

2.8 miles:
Former community of Bayview. Had its own post office in 1901.

3.5 miles:
Turn left and drive north on South Beaver Creek Road.

8.8 miles:
Turn left on North Beaver Creek Road. To the right is the site of Ona, which had its own post office in 1890. *Ona* is Chinook jargon for 'razor clam.'

9.9 miles:
Intersection with Highway 101. Turn right and drive north. Ona Beach State Park is on the west side of the highway.

11.6 miles:
Lost Creek State Park, where rock hounds search for blue agates. Winter storms continually cover and uncover these highly desired stones.

11.9 miles:
Site of the former community of Forfar.

13.7 miles:
Newport Municipal Airport.

15.5 miles:
South Beach State Park. Camping, picnicking, and restrooms.

16.3 miles:
Newport

Newport

Yaquina Bay Bridge

Elevation: 87 feet

Location:
44.37.416 N • 124.03.800 W

Services:
gas, food, lodging, B&B, RV

In 1855, much of what would become Lincoln County was designated as a reservation for Native Americans. Then, as settlers began arriving, the land was slowly taken away from the Indians. Olsonville, today enveloped by Newport, was a community on the shore near the bay, and the 1856 site of Lt. Phil Sheridan's blockhouse. Olson was named after sea captain Olson Johnson who came here in 1861. Yaquina Bay opened to settlement in 1864 and thrived by selling oysters to gold miners in San Francisco and to wealthy New Yorkers at the Waldorf-Astoria Hotel. The Newport post office opened in 1868 and the town was incorporated in 1882. Lincoln County was established in 1883 and Newport became the county seat. Highway 101, or the Roosevelt Military Highway, was constructed, county-by-county, between 1919 and 1936. 1936 is also the year the Yaquina Bridge was opened. Newport is home to the Hatfield Marine Science Center, which opened in 1965.

Points of Interest

- **Historic Bay Front** *(Bay Boulevard between Harbor Street and John Moore Drive)*
  Early location of Newport commerce. Old buildings have signs explaining their heritage.

- **Burrows House Museum** *(545 SW 9th)*
  Built in 1895, this Victorian home is full of period pieces and information about early Newport.

- **Oregon Coast History Center** *(545 SW 9th)*
  Adjacent to the Burrow's house is the old log cabin museum.

- **Barge Inn** *(358 Bay)*
  Constructed in 1905.

- **Bay Haven Inn** *(620 Bay)*
  Opened 1886.

- **Mo's Clam Chowder** *(622 Bay)*
  The successful restaurant chain started in this 1912 garage.

- **Old Newport Bank** *(Fall and Bay)*
  1912 construction.

- **Nye Beach** *(between 1st and 10th and Coast Street)*
  A favorite area for tourists since the 1900s. Many old Victorian homes in this area.

- **Nye Beach Hotel** *(219 NW Cliff)*
  Built in 1910.

Nye Beach

- **Dr. Henry Minthorn House**
  (231 Cliff Street)
  The uncle of Herbert Hoover built this home in 1902.

- **Sylvia Beach Hotel**
  (267 NW Cliff)
  Rooms are named after authors and their works, such as the Edgar Allen Poe Pit and the Pendulum room, complete with a giant broad ax embedded in the ceiling. Built around 1912.

- **Yaquina Art Association**
  (839 NW Beach Drive)
  In 1905, Sam Irvin built this as a natatorium, theater and dance hall. It is now the art center.

- **Yaquina Bay Lighthouse and State Park** *(Government Street)*
  Built in 1871, this is the only wooden lighthouse on the Oregon Coast. It is the oldest building in Newport and allegedly haunted.

- **South Jetty** *(by the bridge)*
  The first of the two jetties, built 1881.

- **North Jetty** *(by the bridge)*
  Constructed as a navigation aide in 1888.

- **Hatfield Marine Science Center**
  (2030 Marine Science Drive)
  A research and teaching facility of Oregon State University, named after former Oregon Senator Mark O. Hatfield.

- **Yaquina Head Lighthouse and Natural Area**
  (north of town on Lighthouse Road)
  Constructed in 1873, the beacon is a much stronger light that the one at Yaquina Bay Lighthouse. Hiking trails, interpretive center, whale watching, restrooms, tide pools.

Newport to Toledo

Distance:
12.8 miles

Directions:
From the historic bay front area, go east on Bay Boulevard.

Points En Route

(mileage from the intersection of Fall and SW Bay Boulevard)

0.7 miles:
Intersection with Moore Drive; continue on SW Bay Boulevard.

4.4 miles:
Sawyer's Landing, a boat launch and RV Park. This is the site of Yaquina City, the largest city on the bay in the 1880s. Tourists from the valley would ride the Oregon Pacific Railroad to this point, and then catch ferries into Newport.

6.0 miles:
Across the bay from this point is the site of Oyster City, established in 1865.

7.2 miles:
Oysterville, home to the Oregon Oyster Farm, which opened in 1907..

8.0 miles:
Pilings from an old oyster farm.

8.7 miles:
Near this point was the 1870 home site of the George Luther Boone homestead, one of the finest homes on the bay. George was great-grandson to Daniel Boone.

8.9 miles:
The pilings in the water were for the Oregon Pacific Railroad.

9.0 miles:
Boone Slough, named for 1852 settler George Boone.

9.5 miles:
Craigie Point. In 1866, Scottish immigrant James Craigie took a 42-acre land claim across the river at this point.

10.5 miles:
Criteser Moorage.

10.8 miles:
More railroad pilings.

12.1 miles:
Grand view of Toledo and the mill.

12.8 miles:
Toledo

Toledo

Elevation: 149 feet

Location:
44.07.020 N • 123.56.003 W

Services:
gas, food, lodging

Early settler, Joseph Graham, named Toledo after his home in Toledo, Ohio. Graham settled here in 1866. The post office opened in 1868 and rapidly grew during World War I when spruce was milled to build airplanes. The Corvallis and Yaquina Bay Railroad came through town in 1885, opening the way for the lumber industry. By 1890 Toledo had a waterfront hotel, saloon, feed stable, blacksmith shop, mercantile and two churches. The town was incorporated for one day in 1893 and officially became a city in 1905. In 1915 it was the largest spruce mill in the world, producing 400,000 board feet of lumber every eight hours. Spruce milled here was used to build Howard Hughes' "Spruce Goose." Toledo is the only inland coastal city with a deep water channel. Summer temperatures in Toledo are 10-15 degrees warmer than Newport.

Toledo

Points of Interest

- **Toledo History Museum**
  (208 N Main)
  A 1939 Art Deco building that is part of the Toledo City Hall.

- **Yaquina Bay Hotel**
  (Graham and Main)
  Toledo's oldest hotel, still in use.

- **United Methodist Church**
  (3rd and Beach)
  Built in 1936.

- **Historic Rail Equipment Display** *(NW 1st)*
  Displays include a 1907 caboose, a mail car, and a 1922 steam engine named "One Spot."

- **St. John's Episcopal Church**
  (110 NE Alder)
  Constructed in 1938.

- **Pacific Spruce Tenant Cottages**
  (NE 6th between Main and Alder)
  These were 1920 homes for the mill workers.

United Methodist Church

Toledo to Elk City

Distance:
10.0 miles

Directions:
Go south on Butler Bridge Road and follow the Yaquina River.

Points En Route

(mileage from Butler Bridge Road and NW 1st)

0.5 miles:
Georgia Pacific Pulp and Paper

0.7 miles:
Keep right on Butler Bridge Rd.

1.0 miles:
Crossing the Yaquina River.

1.4 miles:
Veer left onto Elk City Road.

3.1 miles:
Old two-story farmhouse that overlooks the river.

4.0 miles:
Salt marsh restoration project.

4.1 miles:
Boat launch, picnic area, restrooms.

7.2 miles:
Site of Burpee.

10.0 miles:
Elk City

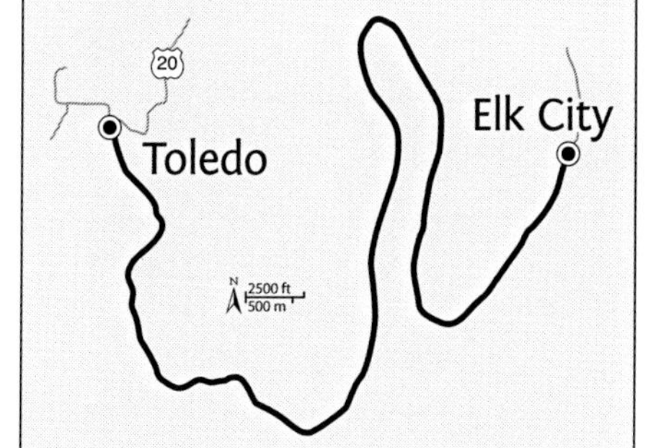

Elk City

Elevation: 150 feet

Location:
44.37.216 N • 123.52.531 W

Services:
none

Elk City is located at the confluence of the Yaquina River and Elk Creek. The Yaquina Bay Wagon Road Company built a warehouse here in 1866. In 1868, the post office opened and the town was platted, both under the name of Newton. The railroad came to town in 1885. The name was changed to Elk City in 1888 because large number of elk roamed the area. Travelers to the coast would come by stage to Elk City and then take a boat to Newport, as Elk City was the terminus for small boat navigation. Elk City flourished as a community until the railroad declined. A covered bridge once spanned the river near the park, falling victim to winds and flood in 1981.

Elk City Grange Hall

Points of Interest

- **Elk City Store** *(Carter Street)*
  Unoccupied and for sale.

- **Elk City Park** *(near the River)*
  Restrooms, picnic, campground, and boat launch.

- **Elk City Grange Hall #515** *(corner of Elk City Road and Simpson)*
  Vacant and withering from little use and lack of maintenance.

- **Elk City School** *(one block off Carter and Simpson)*
  The 1921 school is now a private residence.

- **Elk City Cemetery**
  Dating to the 1893, the cemetery is located on Big Harlan Road.

Elk City to Chitwood

Distance:
7.5 miles

Directions:
From the Elk City Park, travel northeast toward Chitwood.

Points En Route

(mileage from the Elk City Park)

0.1 miles:
Pavement ends, 4.9 miles of graveled road begins.

0.5 miles:
Old homestead.

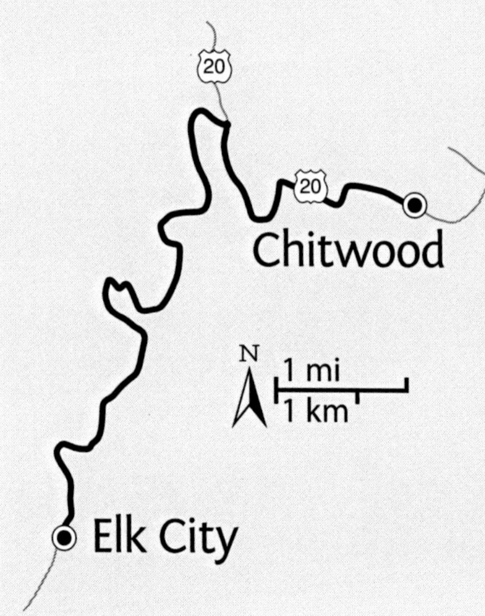

1.3 miles:
Private foot bridge.

2.1 miles:
Remains of an old orchard and site of Pioneer, which had its own post office in 1868. The community of Pioneer was once named Morrison, after its first postmaster. Pioneer received its name from the Pioneer Sandstone Company.

2.5 miles:
Crossing the Yaquina River.

3.4 miles:
One lane traffic with a twelve-foot clearance.

4.0 miles:
Railroad tunnel to the right.

4.9 miles:
Pavement returns.

5.0 miles:
Intersection with Highway 20. Turn right and drive east.

7.5 miles:
Chitwood

Chitwood

Elevation: 90 feet

Location:
44.39.236 N • 123.49.079 W

Services:
none

The first settler came to this area in the 1860s, the railroad came through in 1881, and the first school was built in 1887.The community was named after Joshua Chitwood, long time resident who lived near the tracks. A sandstone quarry produced large quantities of rock for buildings along the coast. The first covered bridge, wide enough for one car, spanned the river in 1893. The current ninety-six foot bridge was constructed in 1926. The Chitwood signs, displayed on both ends of the bridge, came from the old railroad depot that was dismantled in 1940. The Chitwood Cemetery is 0.2 miles east and north of the covered bridge.

Chitwood covered bridge

Chitwood to Eddyville

Distance:
5.0 miles

Directions:
From the covered bridge, drive east on Highway 20.

Points En Route

(mileage from Highway 20 and the covered bridge)

0.1 miles:
River Rest Trailer Park.

4.6 miles:
State Historical marker (between mileposts 22 and 23).

5.0 miles:
Eddyville

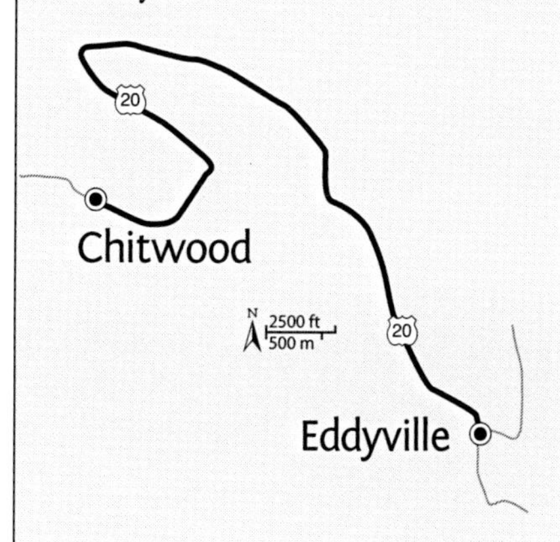

Eddyville

Elevation: 252 feet

Location:
44.38.040 N • 123.46.660 W

Services:
none

Israel Eddy settled in the area in 1870. Eddy was a giant of a man, six feet seven inches tall and weighed 250 pounds. Eddy built a sawmill and a gristmill near the river. The post office opened in 1888 under the name Little Elk, but was changed to Eddyville in 1900 when the post office moved to the home of postmaster and town founder Israel Eddy. Eddyville is near the confluence of the Yaquina River and Little Elk Creek. Eddyville is home to the Rain Forest Mushroom Company.

bridge in Eddyville

Points of Interest

- **Eddyville School**
  Constructed in 1915.

- **Eddyville Log Cabin Museum**
  Located on the school grounds (rarely open).

- **Eddyville Post Office**
  The modern office is located at the junction of Highway 20 and the Eddyville-Blodgett Highway.

Eddyville School

Eddyville to Blodgett

Distance:
20.8 miles

Directions:
From the post office, drive east on Eddyville-Blodgett Road.

Points En Route

(mileage from the post office)

2.3 miles:
Railroad crossing, one of several along this route.

2.4 miles:
Crossing the Yaquina River.

4.5 miles:
Dilapidated and abandoned home.

5.1 miles:
Community of Nortons, named for the pioneer family who first lived and farmed here. Nortons had a post office in 1895.

9.9 miles:
Abandoned home.

10.9 miles:
Turn right on Clem Road. Go under the railroad trestle. 4.1 miles of well maintained gravel begins.

11.2 miles:
One-lane bridge.

11.6 miles:
Crossing Young Creek.

12.6 miles:
Logging camp.

15.0 miles:
Pavement returns.

15.1 miles:
RV Park.

15.2 miles:
Intersection with Highway 20. Turn left and drive east toward Blodgett.

16.3 miles:
Entering Benton County.

18.6 miles:
Turn right on Old Blodgett Road, traveling south.

20.8 miles:
Blodgett

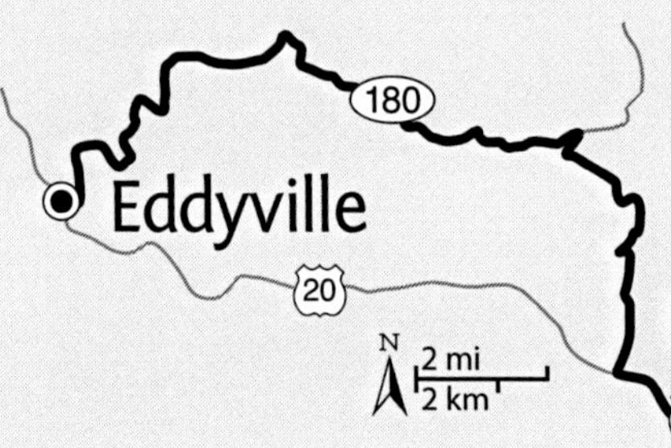

Blodgett

Elevation: 591 feet

Location:
44.35.526 N • 123.31.713 W

Services:
gas, food

Located on the banks of Mary's River, the community's first post office opened in 1888 under the name of Emrick, in honor of a local pioneer family. The post office was housed in the general store, which was built the same year. The name was changed to Blodgett to honor William Blodgett, another pioneer resident. Blodgett is part of the Philomath School District.

Points of Interest

- **Blodgett School** *(corner of Old Blodgett Road and Tum Tum Lane)*
  The first school was constructed in 1850; this one in 1929.

- **Blodgett Country Store** *(on Highway 20)*
  Built in 1888, the walls of the old store display unique photos of the community as it looked years ago.

covered bridge between Blodgett and Wren

Blodgett to Wren

Distance:
7.8 miles

Directions:
At the intersection of Blodgett Road and Tum Tum, turn left onto Tum Tum, and drive south toward Wren.

Points En Route

(mileage from the intersection of Blodgett and Tum Tum)

0.1 miles:
Pavement ends. 5.1 miles of gravel.

0.4 miles:
Turn left on Harris Road.

0.6 miles:
Unusual house crafted out of cement.

1.9 miles:
Railroad crossing and stop sign.

3.0 miles:
One-lane bridge.

3.4 miles:
Morgan Manor, an equestrian facility for thoroughbred Morgan horses.

5.2 miles:
Pavement returns.

5.3 miles:
The 1923 Harris Covered Bridge that spans the Mary's River.

5.3 miles:
House with two front doors.

5.4 miles:
Harris Covered Bridge Winery and tasting room.

5.5 miles:
Pavement ends. 1.0 miles of gravel follow.

5.6 miles:
A large, old home near the RR tracks was part of the former community of Harris, settled in 1890 by the Harris family.

6.5 miles:
Pavement returns.

7.1 miles:
An abandoned, log home.

7.8 miles:
Wren

Wren

Elevation: 629 feet

Location:
44.35.264 N • 123.25.600 W

Services:
gas, food

Originally called Wrens, Wren is situated at the junction of Highway 223 and Highway 20. Wren was a stop on the Oregon Pacific Railroad, which operated a station here in 1886. The post office opened in 1887 and closed in 1968. During the peak of the timber industry, numerous mills operated round the clock in this small community, named for an early Benton County pioneer. A scattering of homes and skeletal remains of the mills are all that remain of this once prosperous lumbering community.

Points of Interest

- **Old Mill Site** *(Rittner Road)*
  Site of an old mill that once covered acres of ground. Only one mill operates today.

- **Wren Cemetery**
  0.6 miles from junction of Highway 20 and Highway 223 on a knoll near the Community Church. The cemetery was established in 1857.

- **Dimple Hill**
  (5.0 miles northeast of town)
  Elevation: 1,495 feet.

Wren

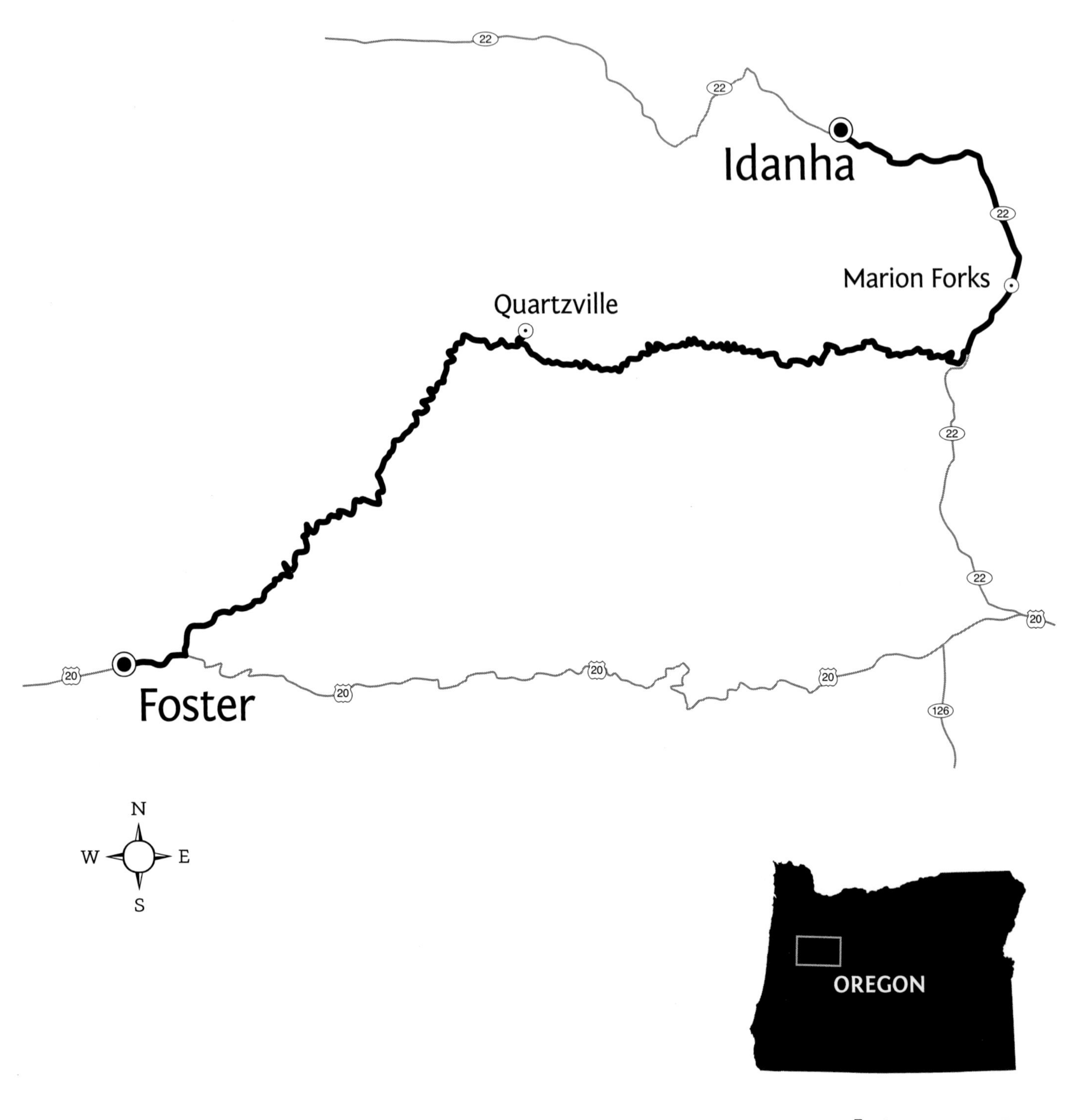

Foster to Idanha

Three Miles of Gold Panning – Yellow Bottom to Quartzville

Foster to Idanha (71 miles)

Experience one of the most peaceful, meandering roads in Oregon on the drive from Foster to Highway 22 along State Forest Road 11. Paved but narrow with numerous pullouts for passing, and lined with campsites, the road over the Cascades is a haven for gold seekers, campers and hikers.

Gas is unavailable on this route, which begins in the small community of Foster and ends in the smaller unincorporated settlement of Idanha. Inquire locally; the road over the mountains is often blocked with snow from November to May.

snow over the road near Quartzville

Foster

Elevation: 569 feet

Location:
44.24.604 N • 122.40.349 W

Services:
gas, food, RV, camping

Foster was named for P.J. Foster, the gristmill owner who used the Santiam River to produce power for manufacturing flour. His mill opened in the 1880s. Hans Wodtli, a Swiss immigrant who settled near the river, built the first hydroelectric plant. Wodtli sold power to residents in Sweet Home and Foster for one dollar per month. Jake Menear was one of the earlier residents of Foster, building a home in 1889. The home stood where Willamette Industries is now located. Foster is a gateway to recreation, with two large reservoirs within eight miles and hundreds of camping sites.

Points of Interest

- **Old Gas Station**
  (Main and 53rd Avenue)
  Built in 1935, the station has been converted into a residence.

- **Foster Elementary School**
  (Poplar and 53rd Avenue)
  This 1921 school replaced the 1892 schoolhouse that stood adjacent to the newer building.

- **Old Santiam Wagon Road**
  (53rd Avenue)
  The old stagecoach road ran from Cascadia to Sweet Home.

- **Foster Cemetery** *(49th Avenue)*
  The cemetery is located on the old stagecoach road and dates to the 1890s.

- **Andrew Wiley Park**
  (53rd Avenue, north of Main)
  Restrooms, picnic area, fishing, and playground. Excellent view of the dam. Fish ladders are located near the playground.

- **Foster Post Office**
  (Poplar and 53rd)
  The new office replaced the one constructed in 1898.

- **Foster Dam** *(end of 53rd Avenue adjacent to Wiley Park)*
  Constructed in 1966, Foster Dam provides flood control, power, irrigation and recreation.

- **Victory Faith Fellowship**
  (Poplar and 54th)
  One of Fosters earliest churches.

Foster Dam

Foster to Quartzville

Distance:
30.0 miles

Directions:
From the intersection of 54th and Main, proceed east on Main (Highway 20).

Points En Route

(mileage from 54th and Main, the Lakeside Market and Deli)

0.1 miles:
Foster Mall.

0.4 miles:
Foster Lake.

0.7 miles:
Foster Lake RV resort.

0.8 miles:
Viewpoint and overlook.

2.6 miles:
Turn left on Quartzville Road.

2.8 miles:
Bridge over Quartzville Creek.

3.7 miles:
Lewis Creek Park.

3.9 miles:
Old Sunnyside School, now a head start facility.

4.0 miles:
Fish hatchery.

4.1 miles:
Sunnyside County Park. Campground and boat launch.

4.3 miles:
Greenhorn Hill, to the left.

4.8 miles:
From here, the road that parallels Quartzville Creek is narrow and winding and with many pullouts.

7.7 miles:
Green Peter Dam and Lake. Green Peter is a combination of names, Green for the color of the forests and Peter, Latin for rock. This dam was constructed in 1962, five years before Foster Dam was built.

8.1 miles:
Basalt Cliffs and views of the reservoir.

8.2 miles:
Camping is permitted along the road in designated areas. Fire pits identify sites.

12.1 miles:
Thistle Creek Park. Boat launch, picnic area, and restrooms. Day use only.

12.9 miles:
Adjacent to the bridge is a pull out with restrooms.

13.8 miles:
Whitcomb Creek Park, maintained by Linn County.

14.7 miles:
Paved road narrows. Good views of the reservoir.

15.6 miles:
Interesting 'rock pillar' on left.

15.7 miles:
The road narrows again.

17.4 miles:
Boat launch.

17.7 miles:
Large parking area, restrooms.

18.7 miles:
Camping area, pit toilets, water.

19.4 miles:
Entering Quartzville Creek National Wild and Scenic River area.

19.9 miles:
Waterfall to the left.

20.8 miles:
Dogwood Picnic Area. A Department of the Interior BLM Park. Restrooms and trail to Cascade Falls.

22.8 miles:
Bridge to the right leads to camping.

25.2 miles:
Crossing Quartzville River.

26.4 miles:
Yellow Bottom Recreation Area. Yellow Bottom is where gold was first discovered in the 1860s. Camping on both sides of the road, restrooms.

27.0 miles:
Small camping area.

27.5 miles:
Additional camping with primitive restrooms. There is a group camp called "Old Miners Meadow,' named for the encampment of gold seekers that once lived here.

27.8 miles:
Bridge. Y in road, stay right.

27.9 miles:
Turn left onto Forest Road 1133. The next 2.1 miles are gravel.

30.0 miles:
Quartzville

Quartzville
N
2 mi
2 km
20
Foster

panning for gold at Yellow Bottom

Quartzville

Elevation: 5123 feet

Location:
44.35.250 N • 122.19.194 W

Services:
none

Jeremiah Driggs first discovered gold here in 1863; the town was platted and a stamp mill constructed by 1864. Quartzville Creek, one of the largest tributaries of the Santiam River, gave the mining community its name. More than 1,000 people and half as many gold claims covered this area until the gold played out in the 1870s. The post office opened in 1888, with George Whitcomb as postmaster. Whitcomb also provided miners with the necessary pack and mining equipment. A new discovery in the 1890s saw a second and smaller rush of miners, only to end by 1902. A stamp mill, temporary stores, saloons and cabins were constructed for the miners. Nothing remains of the boomtown community except for mining claim tailings and hard rock mine shafts. During the two short-lived booms, approximately $200,000 worth of gold was removed from the creeks. Treasure hunters can frequently be seen using metal detectors to locate objects lost by the miners.

Points of Interest

- **Site of Quartzville**
  Hike the old creek bed and drive east and west of the town site. Imagine miners seeking their fortunes at this mile high community.

Quartzville to Marion Forks

Distance:
29.4 miles

Directions:
Return to the intersection of Forest Road 1133 and Forest Road 11. Turn Left.

Points En Route

(mileage from the "Road Closed" section of road off of Forest Road 1133)

2.1 miles:
Turn left and drive east on Forest Road 11.

2.8 miles:
End of recreational mining.

3.7 miles:
Parking, bridge and campsites.

3.9 miles:
Pullout and view of Quartzville Creek.

4.1 miles:
Primitive campsites.

4.2 miles:
More campsites and firepots.

4.5 miles:
Camping sites.

4.7 miles:
Large camp area and McQuade Creek Trailhead.

4.9 miles:
Bridge over the river.

5.4 miles:
First of many mining claims, this one identified as Market Claim.

6.7 miles:
Bridge.

7.1 miles:
Unique rock formation.

8.1 miles:
Another bridge over Quartzville Creek.

site of Quartzville

9.4 miles:
Intersection with Forest Road 1155. Stay on Forest Road 11.

12.7 miles:
Forest Road 11 meets Forest Road 740. Stay on Forest Road 11.

13.1 miles:
Stay on Forest Road 11.

13.8 miles:
Continue on Forest Road 11.

16.2 miles:
Forest Road 1133 intersects with Forest Road 11. Stay on Forest Road 11.

16.3 miles:
Summit.

16.4 miles:
Road joins with Forest Road 1133. Stay on Forest Road 11.

17.0 miles:
Waterfall on right.

17.4 miles:
Views of the valley.

20.4 miles:
Intersection with Forest Road 10. Proceed on Forest Road 11.

23.4 miles:
Forest Road 11 meets Forest Road 1164. Stay on Forest Road 11.

25.1 miles:
Information kiosk about the Quartzville Scenic Byway.

26.4 miles:
Bridge.

26.5 miles:
Intersection with State Highway 22. Turn left and drive toward Marion Forks and Salem.

26.8 miles:
Paralleling the Santiam River.

27.5 miles:
View of Mt. Jefferson.

29.3 miles:
Marion Forks Fish Hatchery (right).

29.4 miles:
Marion Forks

Quartzville Creek

road to Marion Lake

Marion Forks

Elevation: 5101 feet

Location:
44.36.708 N • 121.56.914 W

Services:
food

Marion Forks is a small community located on the North Santiam River. It was named, as was the county, for Francis Marion, the "Swamp Fox" of Revolutionary War fame. The restaurant was built in the 1980s when the old store and café burned. For many years, the old chimney stood across the highway to commemorate the site of the old store, but it has since been torn down. Hummingbirds abound at the feeders that hang from the restaurant's walls, a treat in summer for diners who take their food on the patio. At the nearby fish hatchery is a trailhead to Marion Lake, known for its small and plentiful rainbow trout.

Marion Forks Restaurant

Points of Interest

- **Marion Forks Fish Hatchery**
  Located across the bridge and close to the highway.

- **Marion Lake**
  An easy hike from the parking area near the hatchery.

road near Marion Forks

Marion Forks to Idanha

Distance:
11.5 miles

Directions:
From the restaurant, travel west toward Idanha.

Points En Route

(mileage from the restaurant)

0.9 miles:
Cross Minto Creek, named for John Minto, pioneer sheep rancher and legislator who came to Oregon in 1844.

2.0 miles:
Riverside Campground, Willamette National Forest.

3.6 miles:
Pamelia Creek. The trail to Pamelia Lake, once an easy hike, was severely damaged because of flooding in 2007.

5.5 miles:
White Water Creek. A national forest campsite constructed in the 1930s.

7.8 miles:
Whispering Falls Campground, another Willamette National Forest site.

9.6 miles:
An old mill site.

11.2 miles:
Another mill site.

11.5 miles:
Idanha

Idanha Community Church

Idanha

Elevation: 1862 feet

Location:
44.42.125 N • 122.04.786 W

Services:
food

Idanha, located on the North Santiam River, was a boomtown when the forest industry was at its peak. Several lumber and plywood mills provided employment for many Santiam Canyon workers. Recreation, camping, fishing and hiking bring people to Idanha. In 2000, over two hundred people lived in the community, with homes located on both sides of the highway. The post office stands near the old grocery store.

Points of Interest

- **Idanha Community Church**
  (397 Church)
  The oldest church in town.

- **Idanha Community Park**
  (395 Church and next to the church)
  Picnic area and primitive facilities.

- **Idanha City Hall**
  (183 Santiam Highway)
  Built in the 1940s.

- **Idanha Store**
  (181 Santiam Highway)
  This market replaced the old store that was destroyed by fire.

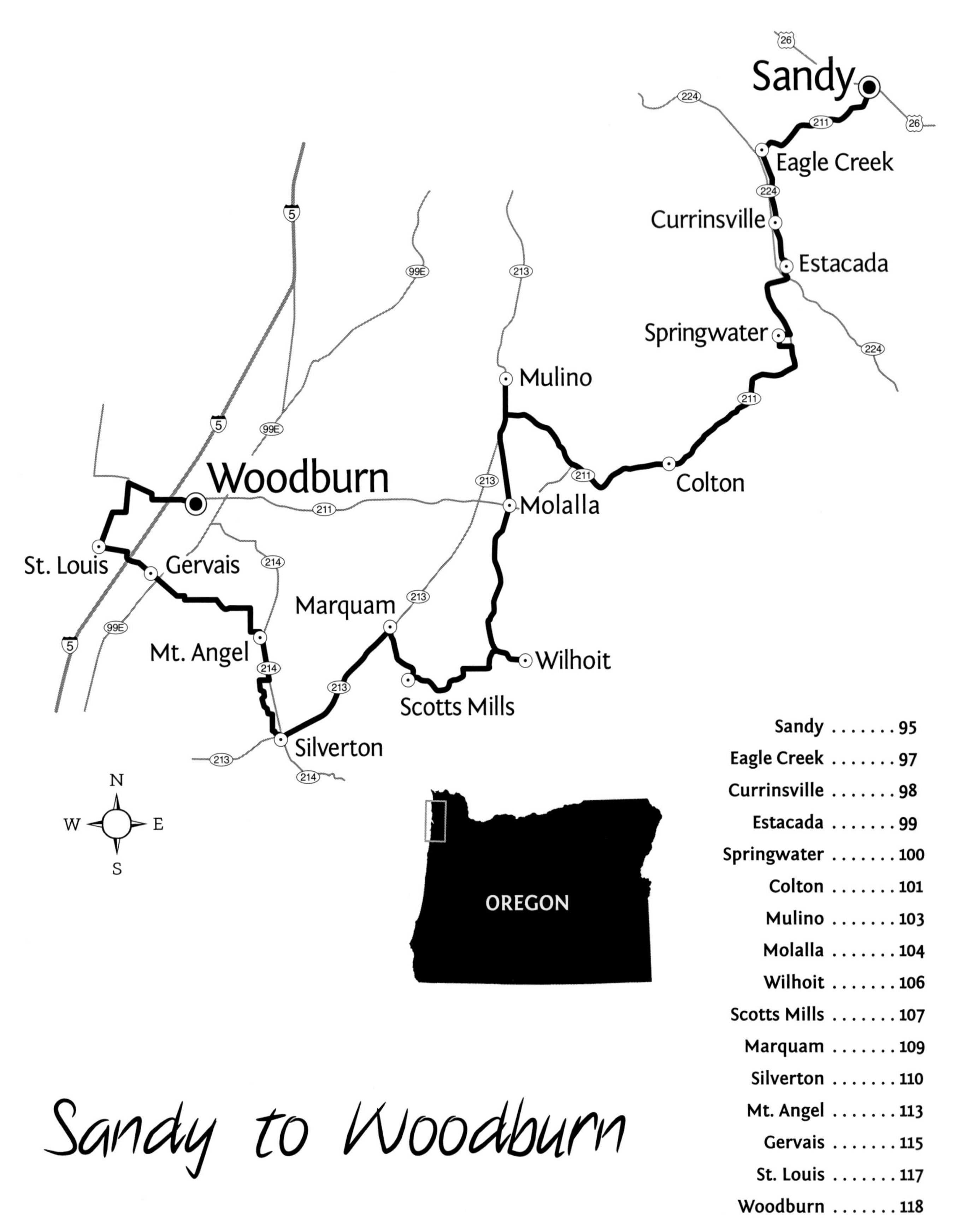

Sandy to Woodburn

Searching for the Devil's Back Bone, Dibble's House and Wilhoit's Spring

Sandy to Woodburn (77 miles)

This route follows the steps of Oregon pioneers along the Barlow Road of the Oregon Trail from Jonsrud Point in Sandy, skirting the foothills of the Cascades and cutting through the heartland of the Willamette Valley.

In addition, hundreds of miles of paved roads, filled with panoramic views and rich with regional history, branch from the scripted route, waiting to be driven and explored. The journey ends in culturally diverse Woodburn, home to large groups of seniors and citizens of Russian and Hispanic origin.

Road Less Traveled near St. Louis

Sandy

Elevation: 988 feet

Location:
45.23.517 N • 122.15.591 W

Services:
gas, food, lodging, B&B

view from Jonsrud Point

Located on the Sandy River, originally named Quicksand River by Lewis and Clark, many pioneers ended the arduous westward journey on the Oregon Trail in Sandy. Sandy was once called Revenue in honor of 1853 settlers Frances and Lydia Revenue, who provided many pioneers with meals and supplies. The area's first school was constructed in 1868, the post office opened in 1873, and the town was incorporated in 1913. Major fires in 1913, 1918 and 1923 destroyed many older buildings that have since been replaced. In 1919, before women were given the right to vote in 1920, Sandy elected Blanche Shelley as mayor and Alice Scales and Edna Esson to the city council. Fifteen city and county parks are within the city limits. Sandy, with a population of slightly more than 8,000, is the gateway to recreation on Mt. Hood. Logging and saw milling, which once dominated the economy, have been replaced by light industry, services, and tourism. Agriculture (wineries, nurseries, berries and row crops) has always been an economic mainstay.

Points of Interest

- **Sandy Lutheran School** *(38706 Pioneer)*
  The 1904 school building is now a naturopathic medical clinic. The school sits near the old Presbyterian Church.

- **Evangelical Lutheran Church and Mission** *(38726 Pioneer)*
  The church opened in 1902 on land donated by Casper Junker. The church is next to the old Lutheran School.

- **Sandy Grange** *(38885 Pioneer)*
  At the corner of Pioneer and Bruns.

- **Hoffmann's Meat Market** *(38922 Pioneer)*
  The meat market opened in 1909.

- **Caspar Junker House** *(39010 Pioneer)*
  Constructed in 1908 and near his business building. Note the old sidewalk that went to the former entrance.

- **Site of Revenue Hotel** *(39055 Pioneer)*
  The former location of the 1874 Revenue Hotel.

- **Junker Business Building** *(39070-080-090-100 Pioneer)*
  Caspar Junker constructed this building close to his home in 1914. It housed an ice cream parlor, harness shop, and café. The 1913 fire destroyed the old building that quartered the saloon and livery stable.

- **R.S. Smith Building** *(39150 Pioneer)*
  Bob Smith, former mayor and councilman, sold Briscos, Durants, Stars, Studebakers, Fords, and Chevrolets from this location.

- **Sandy Historical Museum** *(39345 Pioneer)*
  Established in 1926, the new building opened in 2007. The new Civic Plaza is located in front of the museum.

Caspar Junker House

- **Doc Williams House**
  (39550 Pioneer)
  Look for large tree trunks that form part of the old structure. Williams came to Sandy in 1906 and built his home in 1920.

- **Jonsrud Point**
  (Bluff Road past Sandy High School)
  The viewpoint overlooks the Devil's Backbone, the Sandy River, and the site of the Revenue's first homestead.

- **Fir Hill Cemetery** *(on Highway 26 near the west entrance of town)*
  Dates to the 1880s.

- **Cliffside Cemetery**
  (1890 Ten Eyeck Rd)
  Dates to 1889.

- **Mt. Hood Historical Sites**
  (north of town on Highway 26)
  The Oregon Trail's historic Barlow Road skirts this mountain, Oregon's highest, and wagon ruts are visible in several locations near Rhododendron and Government Camp. Barlow's Trail follows Ten Eyck Road and Highway 211 toward Eagle Creek.

Sandy Ridge School

Sandy to Eagle Creek

Distance:
5.8 miles

Directions:
From the intersection of Pioneer and Meinig Avenue, travel southwest on Meinig (Highway 211).

Points En Route

(mileage from the intersection of Pioneer and Meinig/Highway 211)

0.1 miles:
New Meinig Park. The Meinig family, early settlers to the area, donated the land for the park, which has a covered picnic shelter, clean restrooms, and a large play structure. The creek that runs through the park was once mined heavily, and gold seekers have altered its course many times over the last hundred years.

2.2 miles:
The 1925 Sandy Ridge School, now a Head Start facility.

3.9 miles:
Alton Collins Retreat Center.

4.6 miles:
Forrester Cemetery, dating to the 1870s.

5.6 miles:
Eagle Creek Elementary School. The old, two-room schoolhouse is behind the new building.

5.7 miles:
Foster Cemetery. Take SE Eagle Creek Lane to the 1847 cemetery. Philip Foster is buried here, as are Nancy Black and Mary Conditt, nine-year old girls who died of acidosis poisoning on September 7, 1859. Other graves date to the 1840s.

5.8 miles:
Eagle Creek

Eagle Creek

Elevation: 341 feet

Location:
45.21.423 N • 122.21.406 W

Services:
none

Native Americans once marveled at the number of eagles inhabiting the area, thus giving the community its name. A mural of Eagle Creek as it looked years ago is painted on the inside walls of the elementary school. The old 1912 school, which replaced the 1867 log structure, stands next to the modern building. The early school is one of only four two-room schoolhouses still standing in Clackamas County. The house adjacent to the school is one of the few remaining homesteads from the original Eagle Creek community.

Eagle Creek School

Foster Farm

Points of Interest

- **Foster Farm** *(intersection of Highway 211 and Eagle Creek Road)* Beginning in 1846, Philip Foster offered meals and camp to trail weary settlers, and a small community eventually grew up around his farm. The lilac tree the Fosters planted at the farm in 1843 is now the oldest known in Oregon. A couple of old homes from the original community of Eagle Creek still remain and are located across the street from the farm. Today, Foster Farm is host to thousands of schoolchildren and adults for tours and hands-on activities that were part of the daily life of Oregon pioneers. The site is also available for picnics, weddings, and other private celebrations and events.

- **Bonnie Lure State Park** *(on the Clackamas River, 1.0 miles west of Eagle Creek)* Fishing, hiking, picnicking, bird watching, and restrooms.

Eagle Creek to Currinsville

Distance:
3.0 miles

Directions:
From the intersection of Highway 211 and Eagle Creek Road, drive south on Eagle Creek Road toward Currinsville.

Points En Route

(mileage from the intersection of Highway 211 and Eagle Creek Road)

1.0 miles:
Eagle Creek Grange Hall.

1.3 miles:
Crossing Eagle Creek.

3.0 miles:
Currinsville

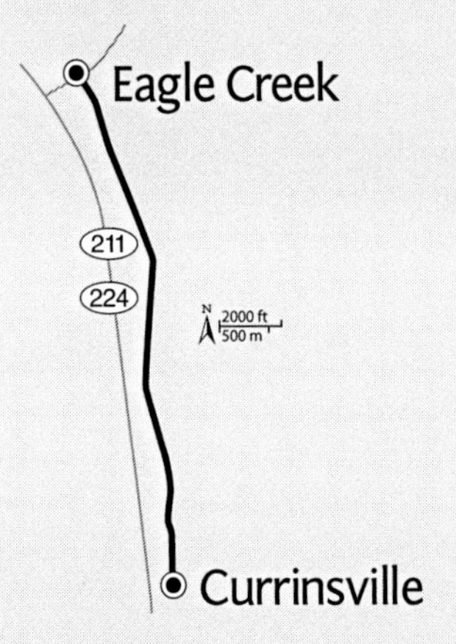

Currinsville

Elevation: 459 feet

Location:
45.19.028 N • 122.20.505 W

Services:
food

Located along the old Portland Electric Rail Line, the town was named for brothers George and Hugh Currin, 1845 pioneer settlers in the area. The first post office opened in 1874 under the name Zion but was changed to Currinsville ten years later. A historical marker, located across the street from the former store, describes the settlement. The Currin brothers are both buried in Foster Cemetery.

Former Currinsville Store

Points of Interest

- **Former Currinsville Store**
  (28424 Eagle Creek)
  Now a restaurant.

- **Old Feed Store**
  (28490 Eagle Creek)
  Next to the restaurant.

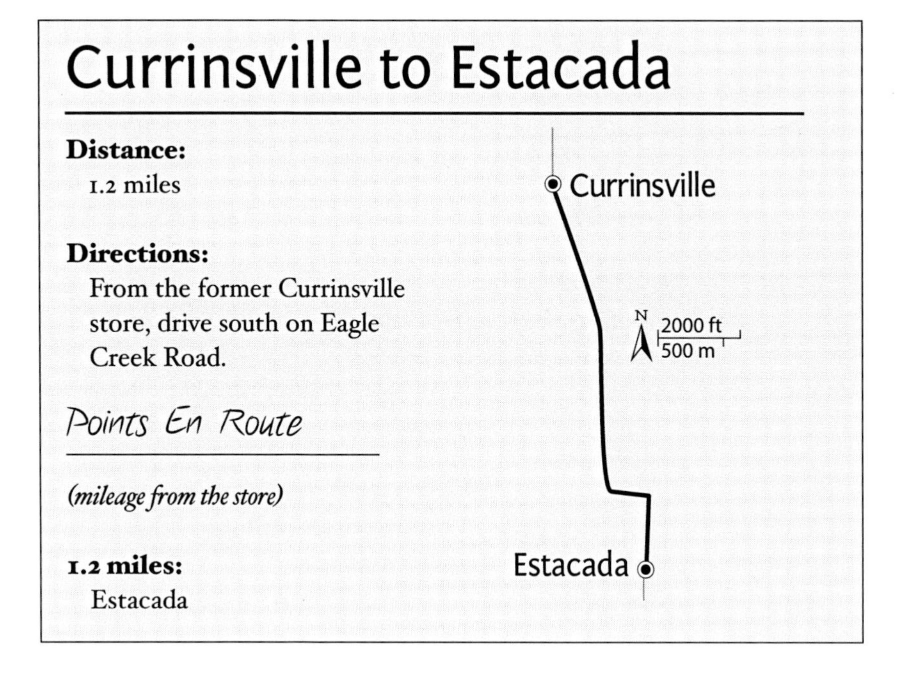

Currinsville to Estacada

Distance:
1.2 miles

Directions:
From the former Currinsville store, drive south on Eagle Creek Road.

Points En Route

(mileage from the store)

1.2 miles:
Estacada

Estacada

Elevation: 472 feet

Location:
45.17.209 N • 122.19.802 W

Services:
gas, food, lodging

Estacada City Hall

Estacada, whose slogan is "Close to everything, but away from it all," was settled in the 1850s but did not incorporate until 1905. The Estacada post office opened in 1904, the same year the Estacada Hotel opened. The hotel, at the terminus of the Oregon Waterway Power Electric Railroad Line, prospered until 1932, four years before it burned to the ground. The name Estacada comes from the Spanish for 'staked out,' describing how the city was platted but having no other historical significance to this community situated on the Clackamas River. Estacada experienced a series of fires that did considerable damage in 1908, 1912, and 1923. The timber industry blossomed in 1923 when the railroad came into town, and in the 1930s Estacada was the state's largest grower of ginseng. Today, Estacada is known as the "Christmas Tree Capital of the World." Since the decline of the timber industry in the 1980s, however, Estacada has slowly become a service oriented, Portland metropolitan area bedroom community. There are fourteen large murals painted on the sides of prominent buildings in the downtown area. The Artback Artists have painted a new mural every year since 1992.

Points of Interest

- **Estacada Methodist Church**
  (204 SE Main)
  The first church was built in 1904 and burned in 1963. The current church was constructed in 1964 on the same site.

- **Chevy and Ford Garages**
  (300 SE Main and 310 SE Main)
  The two agencies were located next door to each other.

- **Estacada City Hall**
  (475 SE Main)
  The City Hall opened in 1905 and was located next to the old Hotel Estacada and the Electric Rail Line. A museum and visitor's center are located adjacent to City Hall.

- **Estacada Fire Department**
  (262 S Broadway)
  The early fire department had two horse carts, 600 feet of hose and forty yards of iron pipe, and was considered "first rate" in its day.

- **Estacada Telephone and Telegraph Building**
  (301 S Broadway)
  Telephones arrived in 1905.

- **Masonic Building**
  (366 SE Broadway)
  Lodge #146 was established in 1911. This building was completed in 1924.

- **Site of Estacada Hospital**
  (103 SW Highway 224)
  The old hospital was located at the corner of Highway 224 and Broadway.

- **McIver State Park**
  (off Springwater Road)
  Covering more than 950 acres, McIver Park offers camping, picnicking, hiking, and fishing. In the 1970s, Oregon's version of the Woodstock rock music festival was held here.

Springwater

Elevation: 1122 feet

Location:
45.15.029 N • 122.20.311 W

Services:
gas, food

The name Springwater comes from a small mineral spring that provided water for a pioneer resident. The local store, church, and grange are reminders of the community's past. The Springwater post office opened in 1874 and closed in 1914. A major fire in 1904 damaged the church and destroyed several other buildings.

Springwater Presbyterian Church

Estacada to Springwater

Distance:
4.0 miles

Directions:
From the intersection of Highway 211 and Broadway, proceed south on Highway 211.

Points En Route

(mileage from the intersection of Highway 211 and Broadway)

0.2 miles:
Veer right, heading south on Highway 211.

1.2 miles:
Road to McIver Park.

3.5 miles:
Turn right on South Wallens Road.

4.0 miles:
Springwater

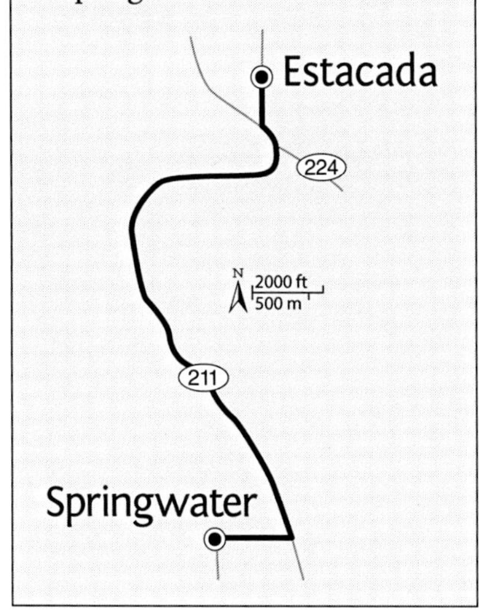

Points of Interest

- **Springwater Grange #263**
  (corner of Springwater and Wallens)
  The 1893 grange sits on the site of the community's first schoolhouse, circa 1870. The school's bell is displayed near the entrance to the grange.

- **Springwater Presbyterian Church** *(next door to the grange)*
  Constructed in 1889. The parsonage is located next door.

- **Springwater Store**
  (next to the church)
  Built in 1930, replacing the 1880s store. The warehouse next to the store was built in 1934.

- **Old Houses**
  (24541 and 24551 Springwater)
  Both survived the fire.

Springwater to Colton

Distance:
9.2 miles

Directions:
From the intersection of South Wallens Road and South Springwater Road, at the Springwater Grange, drive south on South Springwater Road.

Points En Route

(mileage from the Springwater Grange)

0.1 miles:
Century Farm.

0.2 miles:
1874 Guttridge Century Farm.

0.5 miles:
Intersection of South Springwater Road and Metzler Park Road. Veer left, continuing on South Springwater. Located on Clear Creek, Metzler Park offers picnicking, camping, hiking, and fishing.

0.9 miles:
Keep right, continuing on Springwater Road.

2.0 miles:
Intersection with Highway 211. Turn right onto Highway 211.

4.9 miles:
Elwood Road. Site of Elwood, named for Reverend Elwood Sylvanus. The Elwood post office opened in 1892 and closed in 1914.

5.4 miles:
Covered Bridge.

9.0 miles:
An old church.

9.1 miles:
Camp Colton.

9.2 miles:
Colton

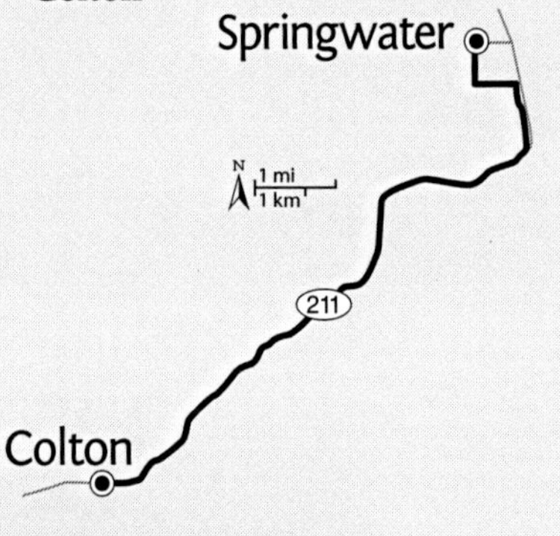

Colton

Elevation: 704 feet

Location:
45.10.327 N • 122.26.121 W

Services:
gas, food

A continual stream of log trucks once made daily deliveries to the local mills in Colton, whose name comes from an early citizen with the last name of Cole. The town was platted in 1892 but never incorporated. At its inception, the community was 100% Swedish. The post office, located near the site of old Colton where the area's first pioneers settled, has been in business more than 100 years. Colton has 172% more earthquake activity than the average community in the United States.

Points of Interest

- **Colton Lutheran Church**
  (Wall and Highway 211)
  The church organized in 1905 and services began in this building in 1907.

- **Colton Lutheran Cemetery**
  (near the church)
  Headstones date to the early 1900s.

- **Colton Market**
  (Wall and Highway 211)
  Opened in 1920.

Colton Lutheran Church

Colton Market

Colton to Mulino

Distance:
10.0 miles

Directions:
From the intersection of Wall and Highway 211, continue south on Highway 211 toward Molalla.

Points En Route

(mileage from the intersection of Wall and Highway 211)

0.6 miles:
Colton Grange, built in the 1920s, served as the hub of this farming and timber community.

2.5 miles:
Camp Colton.

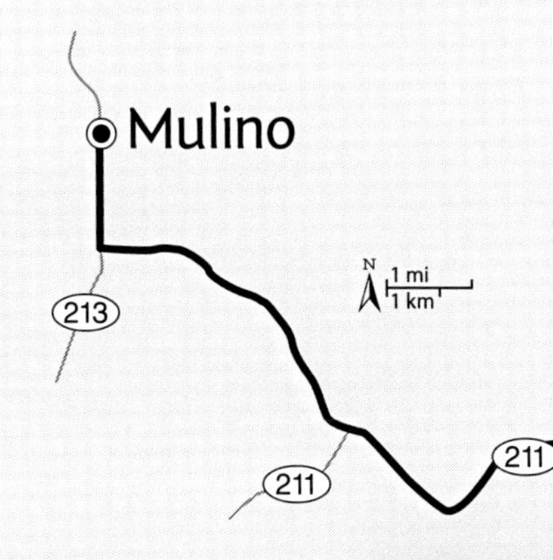

2.9 miles:
Site of Cedardale, former logging community. The old general store is now a carpet and flooring warehouse.

4.5 miles:
Meadowbrook and Country Christian Church and School. Located on Milk Creek, the Meadow Brook post office opened in 1889. The name changed to Meadowbrook in 1895 and the office closed in 1905.

4.6 miles:
Intersection of Highway 211 and Union Mills Road. Take Union Mills Road by driving straight across the intersection. Locals refer to this as "Four Corners."

7.5 miles:
The former Union Mills School.

7.7 miles:
Union Mills. Located on Milk Creek, the mill opened and has continuously operated since 1877. A post office, under the name of Cuttingsville, opened here in 1867. The name was changed to Union Mills in 1875. The original mill burned in 1877 and was quickly rebuilt. Waterpower provided enough energy to operate the sawmill and the flourmill. A century farm stands adjacent to the mill.

7.8 miles:
An old home.

8.7 miles:
Intersection with Highway 213. Turn right, driving north on Highway 213.

9.5 miles:
Remains of the old Mulino school.

10.0 miles:
Mulino

Union Mills

Mulino

Elevation: 243 feet

Location:
45.13.207 N • 122.34.809 W

Services:
gas, food, B&B

In 1875, the name Mulino was derived from the Spanish word *molino*, which means, 'mill.' The community was originally known as "Howard's Mill," named after the owner and operator of the 1851 flourmill. The post office has operated continuously since 1882, yet the town was not platted until 1912. In 2007, residents voted to give Mulino "Hamlet status," which means a small community surrounding a place of work or worship.

Howard's Grist Mill

Points of Interest

- **Howard's Grist Mill**
  (north of the intersection of Mulino Road and Highway 213)
  Howard's Mill, for which the town was originally named, was constructed in 1851 and today has been remodeled into a private residence. The dam that once provided power is behind the mill, and a grain storage building stands across the street.

- **Mulino House**
  (26570 Highway 213)
  The old home, now a Bed and Breakfast, was built in 1887. The current owner is a descendant of the original owner.

- **Howard Cemetery** *(located north of Mulino off of Highway 213)*
  Dates to the 1860s. Howard, the builder/owner of the mill, is buried here.

Mulino to Molalla

Distance:
4.8 miles

Directions:
From the intersection of Mulino Road and Highway 213, backtrack on Highway 213, traveling south toward Molalla.

Points En Route

(mileage from the intersection of Highway 213 and Mulino Road)

1.4 miles:
Crossing the Molalla River.

1.5 miles:
Wagon Wheel Park. Picnic, swim and fish.

1.6 miles:
Arrowhead Golf Course.

1.8 miles:
Liberal. Named for its extreme left wing political views, the area was settled in 1844. The Liberal post office opened in 1893 and was housed in the general store. The new store was built in 1911. The house adjacent to the Liberal Store was built in 1899.

2.3 miles:
Lumber mill.

2.7 miles:
Turn left onto South Molalla Avenue.

4.8 miles:
Molalla

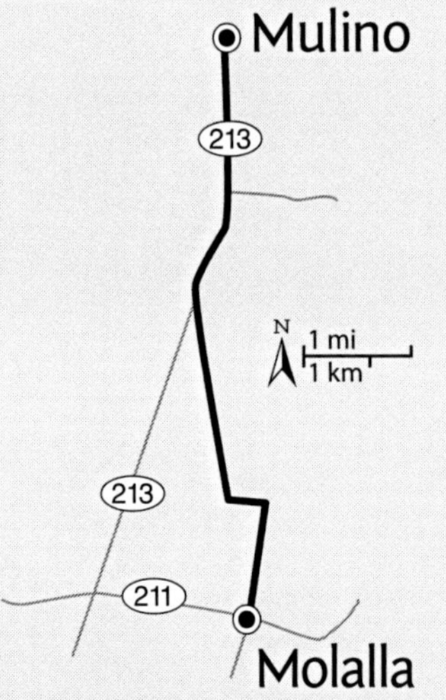

Molalla

Elevation: 374 feet

Location:
45.08.584 N • 122.34.507 W

Services:
gas, food, lodging, B&B

Ivor Davies Hall Museum

The names of the town and the river come from the Native American words *mo* (deer) and *alalla* (berries). The Molalla Indians, of the Wailatpuan tribe of hunters and gatherers and associated with the Cayuse, were the area's first inhabitants. William Vaughn, an 1844 settler, built his home and platted the town at the intersection of two Native American trails. The Molalla post office opened in 1850, the first school held classes in 1856, and the first store opened in 1857. In 1913, Molalla incorporated, printed its first newspaper, opened the telephone company, and received electricity. The railroad came to town in 1913, the year of the first Molalla Buckeroo Rodeo, which has been held every year since. In 1944, a major fire destroyed several downtown business and, in 1993, a 5.7 magnitude earthquake caused considerable damage to many buildings, including the 1926 high school. Today, farming is the major industry where forest products once ruled the economy.

Points of Interest

- **Dibble House** *(616 S Molalla)*
  Constructed in 1859, now part of the Historical Society complex.

- **Von Der Ahe House**
  (part of the historical society complex)
  This 1869 house and former stage stop near Carus was moved to this site in 1972 as part of the museum.

- **Ivor Davies Hall Museum**
  (part of the historical society complex)
  The Hall was constructed of architectural elements from the 1926 Molalla High School that was demolished after the 1993 earthquake.

- **W.W. Everhart House**
  (603 S Molalla)
  The 1913 home of Molalla's first mayor.

- **Everman Robbins House**
  (521 S Molalla)
  A Craftsman bungalow built in 1915.

- **Fox Park** *(between Robbins and Ross on S Molalla)*
  On the site of the old Molalla High School, which had to be demolished after the 1993 earthquake.

- **James F. Adams House**
  (214 S Molalla)
  This home, constructed in 1900, is considered a two-story Foursquare Craftsman.

- **Thomas Ridings House**
  (221 S Molalla)
  Another Craftsman built in 1920.

- **William Adams Building**
  (112-114 S Molalla)
  Built about 1875. Adams was a cabinet and coffin maker.

- **J.H. Vernon House** *(124 3rd)*
  A 1912 example of a Craftsman style home.

- **Dr. Elmer Todd House**
  (102 3rd)
  The doctor was born and raised in Molalla and made "horse and buggy" house calls.

- **Telephone Company Building**
  (115 W Main)
  Opened in 1928 on the site of the 1875 Molalla School.

Molalla

Points of Interest (continued)

- **Albright and Holman Building** *(106-112 W Main)*
  Constructed in 1922 as a Ford dealership.

- **Hoffman House** *(523 E Main)*
  This home was built for Oliver Robbins in 1900 and doubled as Molalla's first library from 1900 to 1906.

- **United Methodist Church** *(300 E Main)*
  Opened in 1905, replacing the old church that stood at the corner of Sawtell and Herman.

- **Everhart Funeral Home** *(220 E Main)*
  Built in 1926.

- **Bowlin Furniture Store** *(118 E Main)*
  Today the White Horse Tavern, the furniture store was the first electrified store in Molalla.

- **Molalla State Bank** *(102-104 E Main)*
  The bank was the first building constructed with fireproof concrete following the city's incorporation. It became the First National Bank in 1918.

- **Levi Wayne House** *(123 Shirley)*
  An example of an 1899 Craftsman. The building behind was a sewing factory for WW II military garments.

- **Larkin-Dibble-Jackson Cemetery** *(off Lowe Road)*
  Located west of town and dates to 1850.

- **Adams Cemetery** *(32840 Adams Road)*
  West of town, past Feyrer Park. Dates to the 1860s.

Von Der Ahe House

United Methodist Church

Molalla State Bank

Wilhoit

Elevation: 747 feet

Location:
45.03.101 N • 122.33.903 W

Services:
pit toilet

Abe and John Larkin discovered the mineral springs in 1847. In 1866, John Wilhoit filed a land claim securing the property and constructed the Wilhoit Springs Resort in the late 1870s. The Wilhoit post office opened in 1882 and the first hotel was constructed in 1886. The resort quickly became an important destination for many people. In 1916 the hotel burned and was replaced by a larger, grander one in 1918. Cabins, an octagonal pavilion, dance hall, general store, and other out buildings were constructed around the hotel and the therapeutic waters. A second fire, in 1920, completely destroyed the new hotel that was never replaced. Deterioration slowly took its toll on the remaining buildings. Nothing remains except for stone foundations, a cistern, and pump for people to taste the water. Wilhoit Mineral Water was bottled and sold in the early 1900s. An information kiosk displays historical photos and offers a glimpse of Wilhoit's heyday. The area is now a park maintained by Clackamas County. Bear are often seen in spring and fall.

Points of Interest

- **Wilhoit Walk**
  A short walk through the park leads past stone outlines of former resort buildings and to the metal-covered cistern of continuously flowing soda water. Take a cup for tasting at the cistern or pump.

Molalla to Wilhoit

Distance:
7.1 miles

Directions:
From the Dibble House, near 6th and Molalla Avenue, drive south on Molalla Avenue toward Wilhoit.

Points En Route

(mileage from the Dibble House)

0.6 miles:
Turn right on S Wilhoit Road.

1.6 miles:
The 1882 Molalla Memorial Cemetery.

5.9 miles:
Intersection of S Wilhoit and S Bird. Continue on S Wilhoit.

7.1 miles:
Wilhoit Springs Park and site of Wilhoit

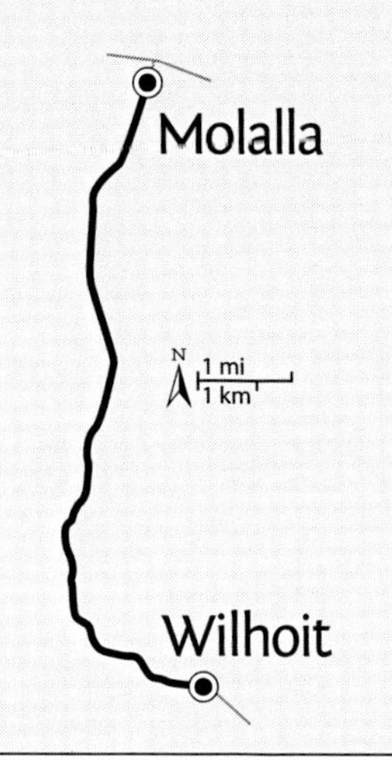

Road to Wilhoit Springs

Wilhoit Springs

Wilhoit to Scotts Mills

Distance:
6.3 miles

Directions:
From the entrance of Wilhoit Springs Park, return west on Wilhoit Road.

Points En Route

(mileage from the park entrance)

1.2 miles:
Intersection with S Bird Road. Turn left on S Bird Road.

2.1 miles:
Old residence and intersection with S Maple Grove Road. Turn right.

3.2 miles:
Intersection with Blair Road. Turn left on Blair Road.

6.2 miles:
Intersection with S Nowlens Bridge Road. Turn left, crossing Butte Creek.

6.3 miles:
Scotts Mills

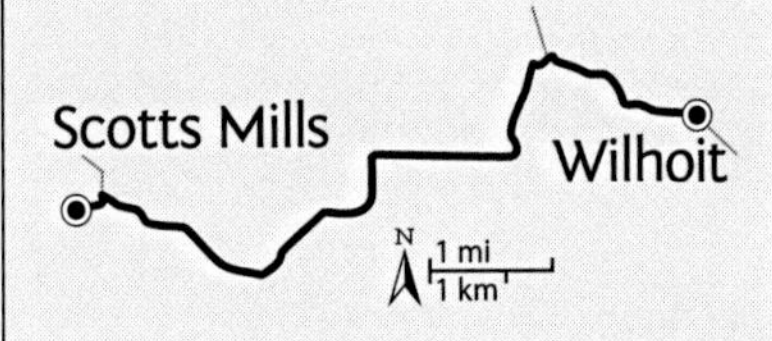

Scotts Mills

Elevation: 423 feet

Location:
45.03.609 N • 122.58.649 W

Services:
food

Thomas McKay, a former Hudson Bay Company employee, and a party of twenty four settlers came to the area in 1846, forming a permanent settlement near Butte Creek. McKay set up a flourmill in 1847 and added a sawmill in 1850, using water from the creek to power the mills. McKay sold the mills to Robert Scott in 1866. Robert Scott, an excellent business mind, made the flour mill the most important mill west of the Mississippi. Robert's son took over the business, which ran into hard times during the depression. The mill was forced to close in the 1930s and was removed in the 1940s. Parts of the concrete dam, used to divert water for power, are visible today. Scotts Mills was named after Robert Scott and his flourmill. The post office opened in 1887, with Robert's brother, Thomas, serving as postmaster. The community was platted in 1893 and incorporated in 1916. Scotts Mills was a center for logging and timber products, which declined in the 1980s.

Old Gristmill foundation

Points of Interest

- **Old Houses**
  150 Grandview; 209 Grandview; 481 Grandview; 698 Grandview; 370 B; 290 C; 102 D; 410 Scott.

- **Scotts Mills Museum and Historical Society**
  (210 Grandview)
  An old church houses artifacts and information. Open one weekend a month.

- **Scotts Mills Bank**
  (300 Grandview)
  The bank opened in 1920.

- **Grange Hall** *(4th and Grandview)*
  Now part of the community center.

- **Friends Church**
  (520 Grand View)
  Built in 1894. The bell can be seen in the tower.

- **Chuck's Gas Station**
  (3rd and Taylor)
  Across the street from the old store.

- **Taylor's General Store**
  (3rd and Taylor)
  The old general store. The old city hall is next door.

- **Scotts Mill Park**
  (4th and Crooked Finger Road)
  Site of the 1846 Thomas McKay gristmill. Restroom, picnic, playground, swimming, and fishing.

- **Old Scotts Mills School**
  (4th and Scott)
  Circa 1916. A private residence.

- **Scotts Mills Cemetery**
  (13277 S Butte Creek Road)
  4.3 miles east on S Butte Creek Road. Dates to the 1860s.

- **Holy Rosary Church**
  (Crooked Finger Road)
  From the park, travel 4.7 miles on Crooked Finger Road. The church dates to 1892.

Chuck's Gas Station

Scotts Mills to Marquam

Distance:
2.5 miles

Directions:
From 3rd and Grandview, return east on 3rd.

Points En Route

(mileage from 3rd and Grandview)

0.1 miles:
Crossing Butte Creek. A covered bridge spanned the creek here until the 1940s.

0.2 miles:
Intersection with Nowlens Bridge Road and S Maple Road. Stay left on Nowlens. Nowlens was an early pioneer in the area and was part owner of the Scotts Mills gristmill.

2.4 miles:
Intersection with Wildcat Road. Keep left on S Nowlens Bridge Road.

2.5 miles:
Marquam

Marquam

Elevation: 295 feet

Location:
45.04.438 N • 122.41.171 W

Services:
food

Marquam is located in the midst of pristine farmland and was once a major producer of hops. The post office opened in 1889 under the name of Butte Creek, but was changed to honor early settler Alfred Marquam. The general store was built in 1878, and was the oldest, continually operating store in Oregon until it closed in 2009. Marquam has never incorporated.

Points of Interest

- **Marquam General Store** *(corner of S Nowlens Bridge Road and Highway 213)*
  The market opened in 1878 and an addition was completed in 1920. Concrete gas pump pads remain from earlier times when gas was sold here.
- **Marquam House** *(corner of Kropf Road and Highway 213)*
  Beautifully restored. Circa 1880.

Marquam House

Marquam to Silverton

Distance:
5.7 miles

Directions:
At the intersection of S Nowlens Bridge Road and Highway 213, drive south on Highway 213 toward Silverton.

Points En Route

(mileage from the intersection of S Nowlens and Highway 213)

0.1 miles:
Marquam Methodist Church (36971 Highway 213) This church opened in 1889 and is surrounded by several older homes. The parsonage, next to church, was built about the same time.

0.8 miles:
Butte Creek School. This newer school, built in the 1940's, replaced the 1907 structure. Named for the nearby creek.

1.8 miles:
Site of Lone Pine. Little remains of this small, agricultural community, located at the intersection of Scotts Mills-Mt. Angel Highway and Highway 213. A two-story general store, demolished in the 1980s, stood at the intersection and provided supplies to travelers and local residents for over eighty years.

Silverton

Elevation: 237 feet

Location:
45.00.241 N • 122.46.572 W

Services:
gas, food, lodging, B&B

The first residents of what is now Silverton were the Ahantchuyuk Indians of the Kalapuya Band. It is estimated that 3,000 Ahantchuyuk lived in the area in 1780. By the 1850s, disease and armed conflict decimated these numbers. Hudson Bay trappers who, inadvertently, brought diseases for which the Native Americans had no immunity, frequented the area in search of beaver from the 1820s to the 1840s. The two-day, 1848 Abiqua conflict with settlers left many Native Americans dead. Silver dollars falling from the saddlebags of a man thrown from his horse and into the creek gave the stream and the town their name. James Brown constructed a leather tannery here in 1846 and the first of several flour mills in the early 1850s. The Silverton post office opened and the town was platted in 1854. By 1868, Silverton boasted three mercantile stores, two gristmills, two blacksmith shops, two wagon shops, a harness and saddle shop, and drugstore. The IOOF and Masons established lodges in 1868, daily stage service to Salem occurred by 1873, and the railroad arrived in 1880. Silverton incorporated in 1885 and the new railroad depot was constructed in 1906. Clark Gable once lived in Silverton and worked as a timber faller in the nearby forests. Agriculture, wineries, artisans, tourism, and services form the economy of Silverton. The Oregon Gardens, built around a 400-year old oak tree, opened in 2000. Walking tour maps of historic Silverton are available at the historical society. Seventeen murals painted on the sides of major buildings help maintain a small town atmosphere. Silverton was home to cartoonist Homer Davenport and a popular summer festival is named after him. Parking meters, in and around town, still take pennies.

Points of Interest

- **All Buildings** *(Main and Water Streets)*
  Silverton's original, downtown commercial area.

- **Wolf Building** *(Main and Water)*
  Constructed in 1891.

- **IOOF Building** *(Main and 1st)*
  Opened in 1915. Three-stories.

- **Masonic Lodge Building** *(Main and 1st)*
  This four-story building opened in 1914.

Train Depot

3.1 miles:
The 1882 Miller Church and 1847 Miller Cemetery. The Miller Church is known as a 'burying church' because it was constructed outside and away from a community with the cemetery its nearest neighbor. The church is uniquely constructed with a twelve-degree pitch to the floor, so the rear of the church is higher than the pulpit area. Pews from the original 1853 structure line the small sanctuary and double doors allow easy display of coffins during funeral services. Note the foundation of the church, balanced on rocks, and exposed to wind and elements.

3.5 miles:
W Abiqua Road. Continue on Highway 213. Abiqua is named for the Native Americans that lived in the area. A battle with settlers occurred in the 1870s near here.

4.2 miles:
Picturesque farmhouse.

5.7 miles:
Silverton

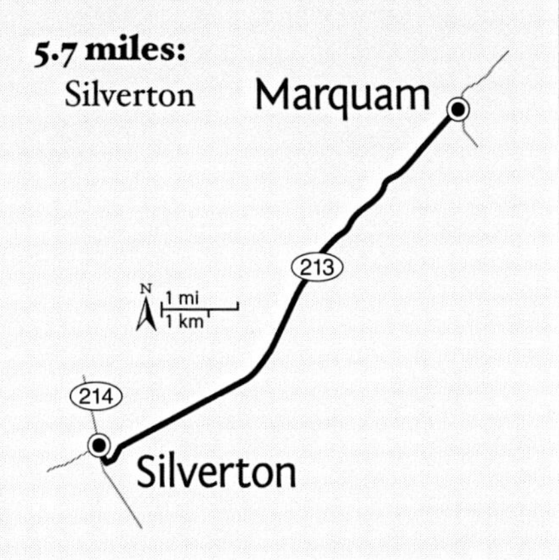

Silverton

Points of Interest (continued)

- **Trinity Lutheran Church** *(500 N 2nd)*
  Built in 1890. Open to the public on Saturdays and Sundays for viewing of the stained glass windows.

- **City Hall** *(Water and Jersey)*
  The two-story structure, built in 1925, replaced the 1885 hall.

- **Frank Wray House** *(403 E Main)*
  Built for the jewelry and furniture storeowner in 1905.

- **Coolidge/McClaine Bank** *(213 E Main)*
  This 1922 bank replaced the original 1890 building.

- **Johnson Building** *(206 E Main)*
  Originally the Silverton Pharmacy.

- **Brooks and Steelhammer Rexall Pharmacy** *(203 E Main)*
  Opened in 1903 and is now a café.

- **Adolphus McClaine House** *(216 W Main)*
  Built by the founder of the bank in 1878.

- **Coolidge House** *(301 W Main)*
  The president of the Silver Falls Lumber Company built this home in 1912.

- **Palace Theater** *(110 N Water)*
  This 1936 theater replaced the 1905 opera house that burned in 1935.

- **Eugene Field School** *(410 N Water)*
  Opened in 1922.

- **Old House** *(417 N Water)*
  Classic two-story bungalow, built circa 1889.

- **Hotel Wolford** *(421 N Water)*
  Now a private residence. Constructed in 1890, near the old railroad depot.

- **Old Hospital** *(1103 N Water)*
  Built in 1890.

- **Silverton Museum** *(428 S Water)*
  Located next to the old train depot, moved from its original location. Across the street is the old Silverton Armory building.

Frank Wray House

Oak Street Building

- **Edward Adams House** *(729 S Water)* Now a B & B.
- **Louis Adams House** *(116 Jerome)* Constructed in 1888. Adams was a lawyer.
- **James and Bessie Smith House** *(119 Fiske)* A Queen Ann built in 1890.
- **W.J. Jerman House** *(105 Grant)* This Hip and Gable home was constructed in 1892.
- **Gunder Ospund House** *(707 E Oak)* Built in 1890 and once served as Silverton's Hospital.
- **Timothy Allen House** *(1006 Pine)* The farmer and creamery owner, born in Silverton in 1854, built his home in 1889.
- **First Christian Church** *(Jersey and 1st)* Constructed in 1889.
- **Silverton Cemetery** *(McClaine and Highway 213)* Dates to the 1850s.
- **Oregon Gardens** *(879 W Main)* An eighty-acre botanical garden and resort.
- **Silver Creek Falls State Park** Travel 15.5 miles west on Water Street. Contains nine waterfalls, most of which are found along a three-mile hike through the park. Several are over 150 feet in height. Hikers are able to walk underneath one of them.

Silverton to Mt. Angel

Distance:
4.4 miles

Directions:
At the four-way stop at S Water and C; drive north on S Water toward Mt. Angel.

Points En Route

(mileage from the intersection of S Water and C)

0.1 miles:
Turn right onto James Street.

0.3 miles:
Old Silverton High School.

0.8 miles:
1902 Brandt Century Farm.

0.9 miles:
Turn left onto Hobart Road.

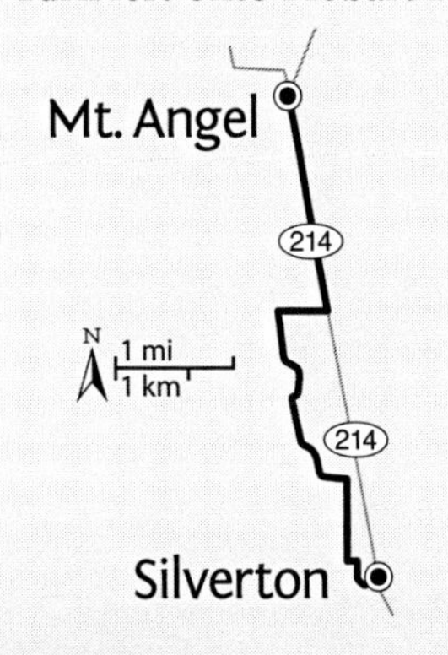

1.1 miles:
St. Paul's Cemetery. Dates to 1870.

1.5 miles:
Turn right on Gallon House Road.

1.9 miles:
Gallon House Covered Bridge. Built in 1916, it is one of the oldest in Oregon and the only covered bridge in Marion County.

2.6 miles:
Intersection of Gallon House Road and Downs. Turn left on Downs. In the distance to the right are views of Mt. Hood and the Benedictine Monastery tucked in the hills above Mt. Angel.

3.1 miles:
Turn right on Mt. Angel Highway.

3.8 miles:
The 1897 Buhr Family Century Farm.

4.4 miles:
Mt. Angel

Gallon House Covered Bridge

Mt. Angel

Elevation: 168 feet

Location:
45.04.018 N • 122.47.904 W

Services:
gas, food

Glockenspiel

The German-Catholic community of Mt. Angel was settled in the 1850s and is named after the 488-foot butte that towers over the city. The community was first called Fillmore, after the president, when the railroad came through in 1880. The railroad station opened in 1881. The post office opened in 1881 under the name of Roy, which was changed to Frankford in 1882, and to Mt. Angel in 1883. The community incorporated in 1893 and received its name from the word *Engelberg* (Angel Mountain Home), a translated version of the Benedictine Monk's home in Switzerland. The Queen of Angels Monastery occupies acres of land near the center of town and Mount Angel Abbey sits high on the hilltop above the town in it's own community of St. Benedict. Mt. Angel's downtown core resembles a quaint, Bavarian village. The spire of the grand St. Mary's Cathedral towers above the landscape in this small farming community of less than 3,000 inhabitants that welcomes over a quarter-million visitors each September to its annual Oktoberfest.

Points of Interest

- **Train Depot** *(Railroad Avenue)*
  Note the large clock tower.

- **Queen of Angels Monastery** *(840 S Main)*
  Established in 1882 by Sisters and postulants from Switzerland and run by the Benedictine Sisters of Mt. Angel. The original building was completed in 1888 and served as a motherhouse and boarding school. Mt. Angel Academy, originally a female charter academy, became Mt. Angel Normal School in 1897 and, subsequently, Mt. Angel Women's College in 1947, then Mt. Angel College in 1957, when it became co-educational. By 1973, following years of financial problems, low enrollment and subsequent loss of accreditation, the Sisters agreed to demands to make the college a Chicano college provided their loan was re-negotiated and re-issued by another party, not the religious order. The name was changed to Colegio Cesar Chavez and various Chicano academicians and students led the short-lived institution. After the closure of Colegio Cesar Chavez, the facilities and grounds were left unused and abandoned for several years. Eventually, a private benefactor purchased the college grounds and facilities and donated them back to the Benedictine Sisters. Today, the former college grounds and facilities are used as St. Joseph Shelter. In partnership with the local community in 1957, the Sisters built the Benedictine Nursing Center adjacent to the Priory. Retreat workshops are offered at the Shalom Prayer Center. Self-guided and guided tours are available and a gift shop and bookstore are open to the public. The Sister's famous mustard can be purchased here.

- **Glockenspiel** *(corner of Charles and Garfield)*
  The four-story glockenspiel is the largest in the United States and sits directly over the Glockenspiel Restaurant and Pub in the Edelweiss Building. The old-world style tower was completed in 2006 in time for the annual Oktoberfest.

- **Weissenfels Blacksmith Shop (Church and Sheridan)**
  A working blacksmith shop, built in 1905.

- **White's Corner Store**
  (Church and Oak)
  Sold groceries and goods into the 1980's.

- **St. Mary's Catholic Church**
  (575 College)
  The grand Cathedral was designed and built in the Revival Gothic style and laid out in the form of a Latin Cross. The church was completed in 1912 and is typified by high, vaulted ceilings with massive ribs, pointed arches and tall, slender, stained-glass windows. It was restored after damage by the 1993 earthquake and is the fourth church built during the first forty years of the Parish.

- **Calvary Cemetery**
  (1015 N Main)
  Dates to 1888.

- **Mount Angel Abbey**
  (One Abbey Drive, St. Benedict, Oregon; at the top of the butte above Mt. Angel, accessed from E. College St.)
  Mount Angel Abbey is a community of Benedictine Monks founded in 1882 from the Abbey of Engelberg in Switzerland. The community of St. Benedict has its own post office, which opened in 1914, and its own cemetery. After establishing their community, the Monks opened Mount Angel College and a seminary. Due to increasing costs and complexity of school operations, the College and its associated high school closed. The Seminary, however, has maintained continuous operation. Visitors may join the Monks in prayer, stroll the grounds past the Romanesque Abbey Church, bell tower and Monastery, and visit the Retreat House, book store, visitors coffee bar and lounge, modest museum and Alvar Aalto Library which houses an original Guttenberg Bible. Spectacular panoramic views of the Willamette Valley are afforded on the Monastery grounds where visitors enjoy the annual Festival of Arts and Wine and Abbey Bach Festival.

- **Zollner Cemetery**
  (North of town on Highway 214, adjacent to creek of same name)
  A family burial plot.

St. Mary's Catholic Church

Mount Angel Abbey

Mt. Angel to Gervais

Distance:
6.1 miles

Directions:
From the intersection of E Church and N Main, drive west on N Main.

Points En Route

(mileage from the intersection of E Church and N Main)

0.1 miles:
Turn right on Lincoln Street.

0.3 miles:
Turn left on W Marquam.

0.5 miles:
Ebner Park. The location for major community celebrations. Playground, sports facilities, restrooms, picnic area.

1.7 miles:
Keep left on Mt. Angel-Gervais Highway.

2.0 miles:
Beautiful farmhouse with a water tower.

2.9 miles:
Crossing the Pudding River.

4.5 miles:
Keep right on Mt. Angel-Gervais Highway.

5.7 miles:
Sacred Heart Cemetery (on the right). Dates to 1834.

5.7 miles:
1875 Masonic Cemetery (on the left).

6.0 miles:
Intersection with Highway 99. Continue straight.

6.1 miles:
Gervais

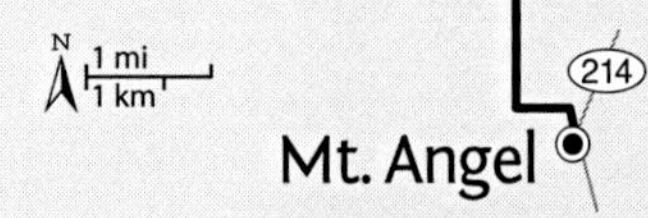

Gervais

Elevation: 180 feet

Location:
45.06.413 N • 122.53.509 W

Services:
food

Gervais is named to honor Joseph Gervais, a fur trapper and member of the Astor settlement, who came to Oregon in 1811. Even though he never resided in Gervais, his name was given to the community. Gervais was said to live in the French Prairie area, but the exact location is not known. In 1843, he was one of the men who voted at Champoeg to establish a provisional government. Sam Brown, pioneer and gold seeker, founded the town in 1850. He built his home, which served as an inn and stagecoach stop in 1858. The railroad came through town in 1870, the same year that the city was platted, and, in 1871, railroad tycoon Ben Holliday donated one block of land for the church. The Sacred Heart Parish was established in 1875 and the city incorporated in 1878. In 1893, the first of several fires occurred, destroying the first church building and many businesses. A second fire occurred in 1894 and yet another fire destroyed much of the downtown in 1902. Only a few buildings were reconstructed after the last fire. One more fire, in 1922, leveled the Sacred Heart Church. The church was rebuilt in 1923 and Sacred Heart School opened in 1955. Butch Cassidy and the Sundance Kid passed through Gervais in the late 1890s, then some years later, notorious killer Harry Tracy. Gervais is a rapidly growing community with agricultural roots and is experiencing a population explosion. Tree farming, dairies, nurseries, and seasonal crops make up the agricultural economy of this small town. The downtown core area parallels the railroad tracks on 4th Street. Large trees, planted long ago, buffer the tracks and the businesses while several older homes stand near the downtown community center.

Gervais Elementary School

Points of Interest

- **Gervais Elementary School**
  (1st and Douglas)
  Constructed as Gervais High School in 1922.

- **Gervais Baptist Church**
  (1st and Douglas)
  Now the Iglesia de Jesucristo Marantha Church.

- **Victorian House** *(325 Elm)*
  Built in 1890 with a hand cranked water pump in the front yard near iron rings used to tie up horses.

- **Gervais Telephone Company**
  (485 3rd)
  Inside the modern facility is the 1938 switchboard.

- **Gervais Market** *(412 4th)*
  Old bottles are displayed on the walls of this 1903 building.

- **Dupuis Building** *(4th and Elm)*
  1902 construction. Opened as the Gervais Tavern.

- **Gervais City Hall** *(524 4th)*
  Located in one of the remaining downtown core buildings.

- **Gervais State Bank** *(542 4th)*
  Built in 1907 and later became part of the original Bank of Oregon. Today it is Catarino Alegria.

- **Bingman Building** *(562 4th)*
  A general merchandise store in 1906 and today the Lucky Fortune Tavern.

- **R.J. Bealey Building** *(592 4th)*
  Constructed in 1902 and housed the Gervais grocery store.

- **Old House** *(720 4th)*
  This 1911 home was constructed after the last fire.

- **Bauman Farms**
  (12989 Howell Prairie Road)
  A family farm market and nursery open year-round, six days a week. Seasonal activities, fresh produce, jams, jellies, gifts, bakery, petting zoo, playground, flowers, plants, garden resources and more.

Brown House

Bauman Farms

Gervais to St. Louis

Distance:
2.6 miles

Directions:
From the intersection of 3rd and Douglas, drive west on Douglas to St. Louis. Douglas Avenue turns into the Gervais-St. Louis Highway.

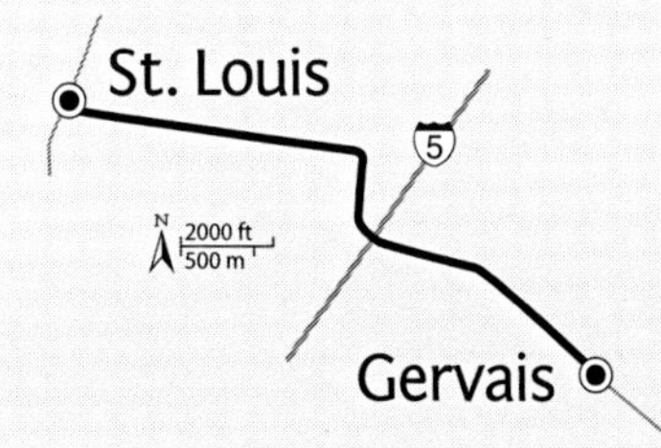

Points En Route

(mileage from 3rd and Douglas)

2.0 miles:
St. Louis Ponds (Tesch Lane). The man-made series of connected, shallow ponds are open March to October for crappie, bluegill, and bass fishing.

2.6 miles:
St. Louis

St. Louis

Elevation: 183 feet

Location:
45.07.213 N • 122.56.324 W

Services:
none

Located at the intersection of St. Louis and Manning Roads, St. Louis is named after King Louis of France, and is the burial site for Marie Dorion, the first white woman settler to travel to the Oregon Territory. En route to Astoria in 1811, Marie gave birth to the first white child born in the new territory. Dorion died in 1850 and is allegedly buried under the existing 1880 Catholic Church, which replaced the 1845 log structure built by Reverend Aloysius Verecuysee. The St. Louis post office operated from 1860 until 1901. Agriculture has always been the economic mainstay of this small community.

St. Louis Catholic Church

Points of Interest

- **St. Louis Cemetery**
  (Dorion Road, west of the church)
  Dates to the 1850s.

- **Church Rectory**
  (on Dorion Road)
  Hand planed log beams, wooden pegs, and grooved boards were used to construct this 150-year-old home.

- **St. Louis Catholic Church**
  (Manning Road)
  This 1880 building replaced the original 1845 log structure. A date on the stained glass windows reads 1847 and was saved when the first building was torn down.

- **St. Louis School House**
  (across from the Parish Hall on Manning Road)
  The 1906 school is now a private residence.

St. Louis to Woodburn

Distance:
4.6 miles

Directions:
From the intersection of Manning Road and Dorion, proceed on north on Manning Road.

Points En Route

(mileage from the intersection of Manning and Dorion)

0.1 miles:
St. Louis School.

1.2 miles:
Mt. Hood is clearly visible.

1.9 miles:
Manning Road becomes Arbor Grove Road.

3.1 miles:
Intersection with Highway 219. Turn right on Highway 219.

3.6 miles:
Woodburn Drag Strip.

4.0 miles:
Woodburn Golf Course, developed in 1925 with sand greens.

4.6 miles:
Woodburn

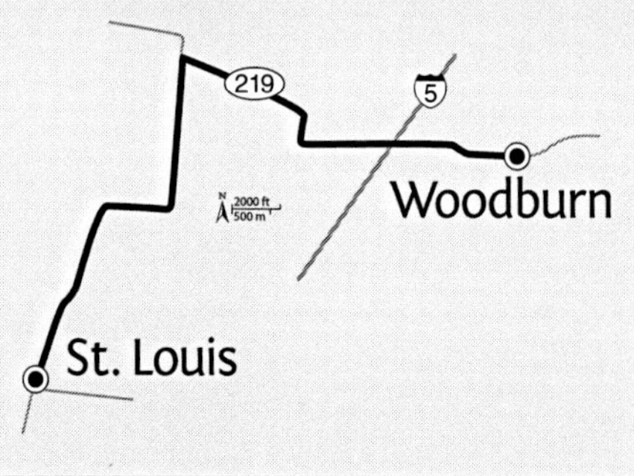

Woodburn

Elevation: 184 feet

Location:
45.08.469 N • 122.51.450 W

Services:
gas, food, lodging, B&B

Jesse Settlemier Mansion

Settled in the 1850's, the town was platted in 1871 by nurseryman Jesse Settlemier and incorporated in 1889. The Oregon and California Railroad came through Woodburn in 1870, giving rise to its growth. The community allegedly received its name from a slash fire that went out of control, blazing into old growth timber that stood near the railroad line. A local resident, witnessing the fire, responded with two words, *woods burn*, giving rise to the less than glamorous name. Two more fires, one in 1893 and the next in 1896, destroyed many homes and businesses in the downtown area. Once an agricultural community, Woodburn is the second largest community in Marion County. Conveniently located on Interstate 5 between Portland and Salem, Woodburn is populated by a unique blend of Russian, Hispanic and Anglo cultures. In addition, there are over 1500 homes that comprise Senior Estates, a retirement community within Woodburn's boundaries. Agriculture, tourism, services and light industry make up Woodburn's growing economy. Shoppers flock by busloads to Woodburn Company Stores, one of Oregon's most visited tourist attractions, located adjacent to the freeway and soon to be the largest factory outlet in the northwest. Woodburn is home to Oregon Golf Association's championship course and Oregon's only drag strip. The annual Tulip Festival and Mexican Fiesta bring thousands of visitors to the community each spring and summer.

Points of Interest

- **Old Woodburn Hospital** *(302 W Hayes)*
  Opened in 1925, now a vacant office building.

- **Blacksmith Shop** *(211 1st)*
  Home to Valley Manufacturing and Stirrup Company.

- **Old House** *(217 1st)*
  Constructed in 1917.

- **Lonergan House** *(245 1st)*
  Built in 1893, it is one of Woodburn's nicest.

- **Dr. L.W. Guiss House** *(285 1st)*
  Constructed in 1880 and now Daniel's Photography Studio.

- **Woodburn Masonic Lodge** *(145 Arthur)*
  Meetings have been held since 1899.

- **E.H. Hall Undertaker** *(130 Grant)*
  Hall opened the store as the coffin maker and undertaker in 1905. To the left of the undertaker was the Home Bakery.

- **Smallman Hotel** *(367 Cleveland)*
  The 1912 hotel has been converted into apartments.

- **Woodburn Railroad Depot** *(3rd Street)*
  Located on St. Luke Church property, the depot was moved to its present location many years ago.

- **Nathman House** *(479 5th)*
  Constructed in 1910 in the Arts and Crafts style.

Woodburn

Points of Interest (continued)

- **Old House** *(167 Settlemier)*
  Note the carriage house in the back.

- **Tracy Poorman House**
  (199 Settlemier)
  Co-owner of the bank, Colonel Poorman built this home in 1906 for his son Tracy, Jr., who ran the local Pix Theatre.

- **Jesse Settlemier Farmhouse**
  (270 Settlemier)
  Circa 1870. Jesse's first wife took her own life in this home.

- **Jesse Settlemier Mansion**
  (355 Settlemier)
  The fourteen room, 5,000 square foot Victorian/Craftsman Mansion was built in 1892 by town founder Jesse Settlemier on nearly three acres of landscaped grounds. The house is recorded in the National Register of Historic Places and is often rented for weddings and other special events. Public tours are offered the first Sunday of each month.

- **Settlemier Park**
  (400 Settlemier Ave)
  Restrooms, picnic, tennis courts, soccer fields, skate park. Established in the 1880s.

- **Old House** *(648 Harrison)*
  Built in the 1870s, possibly the oldest home in Woodburn.

- **Old House** *(465 Garfield)*
  Constructed in 1900.

- **Dentist House and Office**
  (488 Garfield)
  The dentist built his home and office close to the sidewalk to make his business accessible to the public.

- **Queen Anne Farmhouse**
  (552 Garfield)
  Constructed in 1901 and remodeled in 1993.

Glatt House

Lonergan House

- **Original Woodburn High School** *(777 E Lincoln)*
  The 1915 building is now Washington Grade School. The second story was lost to arson.

- **Locomotive 1785** *(Front and Cleveland)*
  A steam engine built in 1902.

- **Woodburn Aquatic Center** *(190 Oak)*
  Replaced the original outdoor pool in the 1990s.

- **Woodburn Berry Center Museum** *(455 Front)*
  Located in the old downtown and across from the railroad tracks. The 1910 Bungalow Theater, now part of the museum, still shows 'classic first run', silent movies. The museum entrance is highlighted with the arch that once extended over highway 99 at the south end of town.

- **Evenden's Drug Store** *(Front and Hayes)*
  Constructed in 1906.

- **Woodburn State Bank** *(199 Front)*
  Opened in 1906 and is now a tax office.

- **Woodburn Opera House** *(607 Front)*
  The former opera house is now Flomer's Furniture.

- **St. Luke's Church** *(417 Harrison)*
  This church opened in 1933, replacing the 1901 facility. The adjacent St. Luke's School opened in 1949, was destroyed by fire, and rebuilt in 1973.

- **Woodburn Grange Hall** *(891 Settlemier)*
  Constructed in 1912 and built near the old Hall School.

- **St. Luke's Cemetery** *(1679 Front)*
  Established in 1904.

- **Glatt House** *(2551 Boones Ferry)*
  Built in 1854. Local artists sell and display their work in this building.

- **MacLaren School** *(2630 N Pacific Hwy)*
  Formerly known as the Oregon State Training Center for wayward young men, it is now a correctional institute for teens. High fences and razor wire surround the facility established in 1891 that once housed Gary Gilmore and Kip Kinkel.

Woodburn State Bank

Tulip field near Woodburn

About the Author

Author Steve Arndt grew up in rural Independence, Oregon during the state's centennial, a setting that kindled his curiosity about the region's history.

His uncle, William Gilbaugh, now a retired Washington State park ranger and noted northwest photographer, further ignited his passion by occasionally taking Steve on tours of Oregon and Washington back roads and byways.

After earning a degree in elementary education from Oregon College of Education (now Western Oregon University), Steve completed advanced degree coursework in special education at OCE, school administration at Portland State University, and his school superintendent credentials at the University of Oregon. In his 40-year career in education, Steve served various Oregon public schools as teacher and administrator, and completed his last nineteen years in higher education as senior associate professor of teacher education, including ten years as a department chair.

Steve, his wife Diane, and their now-grown children have spent many weekends and school vacations exploring Oregon back roads and off-the-beaten places. Today, their car is filled with child safety seats for young granddaughters that have begun road-trips with grandma and grandpa. Both Steve and Diane continue to fill important roles at the Woodburn United Methodist Church and enjoy volunteering in the Woodburn community and participating in various philanthropic groups and endeavors.

Although Diane, a retired music educator and professional singer, has no formal training in photography, she enjoys her role as photographer, organizer, and proofreader of Steve's book series.